D0730479

TECHNOLOGY AND
INTERNATIONAL RELATIONS

TECHNOLOGY AND INTERNATIONAL RELATIONS

John V. Granger

W. H. FREEMAN AND COMPANY
SAN FRANCISCO

Library of Congress Cataloging in Publication Data

Granger, John Van Nuys, 1918–
    Technology and international relations.

    Includes index.
    1. International relations.
2. Technology—International cooperation.
3. Technology and state.
I. Title.
JX1255.G74 327 78-15363
ISBN 0–7167–1004–8
ISBN 0–7167–1003–X pbk.

9 8 7 6 5 4 3 2 1

CONTENTS

This is for my wife, whose patience made it possible.

PREFACE

The purposes of this book are several. The first is to describe the nature of modern technology, the ways it comes into being, its potentials and limitations, and how the technological enterprise is organized and operated by governments and industry. A second purpose is to show how governments seek, individually and collectively, to direct and regulate the uses, impacts, and international flows of technology, and the political effects these activities have on various elements of society. Yet another purpose is to illustrate the pervasiveness and complexity of international technological interdependence, and the public policy issues it raises, by examples in the areas of trade and investment, national security, and development assistance. The areas chosen for consideration are by no means comprehensive; some important ones are omitted altogether. The examples included will, however, give the reader a general comprehension of the various ways in which the issues that confront our nation and others in the international arena so often link importantly to technological factors.

Throughout these discussions, I have attempted to identify obstacles to successful policy formulation and other effective responses to recurring problems and to suggest ways of strengthening the capabilities of governments—particularly our own—and of international organizations in dealing with these matters.

Many books and countless articles in popular magazines and scholarly journals have taken up some or all of these topics. Why another book, then? I undertook this volume because the texts that have dealt at all comprehensively with the relationship of technology and foreign affairs are sadly out of date—no surprise in an area where things change so rapidly. Excellent coverage of specialized topics is available, of course, but the reader who seeks a cohesive approach, an organizing idea, in this literature will search in vain. Finally, I know of no comprehensive effort to describe the many-faceted interactions between government and industry that are the overriding reality of this sphere.

The United States, indeed the whole world, faces enormous challenges in the years ahead. Technology, with its promises and its failures, is a central factor in international relations. I hope that this volume will shed some light as men and women of good will, in government, in industry, in the universities, in international organizations, or simply bewildered before their television sets, seek a path to a better world.

For want of a better place to say it, I will declare here my basic attitudinal bias. I am an optimist. In a time that embraces too many wars, hot and cold, my personal experience with the characteristic conflicts of international relations convinces me that the vast majority of peoples everywhere—and their leaders—prefer peace, wish to achieve their goals in harmony with others, and accept the necessity of cooperation in the pursuit of the common good. Faulty conceptions, poor communications, and the exigencies of difficult and often intolerable circumstances color international relations as they do interpersonal ones, but with patience and fortitude these problems can be overcome. If this does not occur in our lifetime, then it will in those of the coming generations, whose lives our decisions and actions will do much to shape.

A few words about terminology: I have chosen to employ in the title of this book and generally throughout the text *international* as a generic adjective, following the common usage, as in *international travel*. In my usage, then, the term subsumes a variety of other terms, some broader (e.g., *foreign*) and others more precise (e.g., *intergovernmental, multinational,* or *transnational*). Where context does not serve to clarify the particular sense intended, I have tried to employ a more precise term, within the limits of practicality. (I have left *international travel* untouched, for example, though it is not the travel of nations that is meant; a literal interpretation of a possibly more exact adjective—*transnational*—would create nonsense.) By extension, I use *international relations* as a catchall, embracing the traditional province of "foreign affairs" and much more as well.

It has been my great good fortune to have come to know and work with some exceptionally wise and experienced people, in and out of government, both in the United States and abroad. I am indebted to each of them for what I have learned about the matters dealt with in this book; without active assistance from many of them, I could not have undertaken to write it. A list of these individuals would be too long to repeat. For those whose assistance and encouragement were crucial throughout and who undertook to review earlier versions or parts or all of the manuscript, I record their names (alphabetically, in the best traditions of science) as a minimal recompense: Mary M. Allen, Gaston Chingari, Herbert Fusfeld, Wreatham Gathright, John Logsdon, Hylan Lyon, Herman Pollack, and Nelson Sievering. If credit is due, a lion's share is theirs. Blame I reserve to myself. A particular mention is due my editor, Ms. Susan Weisberg, whose careful blue penciling contributed much to clarity and accuracy, and to Ms. Patricia Niner, who persisted with organizing and reorganizing the typing even when the cause seemed lost.

August 1978   *John V. Granger*
London

INTRODUCTION

Technology has created an interdependent world. The process began long ago, when our Neolithic ancestors first learned that a surplus supply of flints for tools and weapons could be traded with others for salt or barley and, as the practice became established, came to rely on such "foreign" sources and to produce for "foreign" consumers. It proved a useful strategy, and as society developed it evolved more sophisticated forms of the strategy. The Phoenicians introduced the economies of scale to overseas trade and built a civilization on the benefits. The British brought Manchester textiles and Sheffield knives to millions previously unaware of a need for either, and relieved the native chiefs of their slow-moving stocks of furs, ivory, tea, and slaves.

With technological advance, villages grew to cities; with the parallel rise of industry and transportation, city states were welded into nation states and the pace of developing interdependence quickened, then surged, then reached breakneck speed. Colonialism emerged as a vehicle for assuring cheap raw materials on the one hand and captive markets on the other. Multinational firms were organized, beginning with the East India Companies and expanding rapidly into mining, manufacturing, and communications. The invention of telegraphy, the undersea cable, and eventually radio quickly demonstrated the need for international protocols and administrative arrangements to insure the technical coordination essential to realizing the benefits of instantaneous international communications.

The pursuit of technology demands resources: human skills, capital, energy and raw materials. A world in which population doubles in three decades while the gap between the rich and the poor continues to widen is already drawing down its nonrenewable reserves of critical materials faster than new sources are being discovered or technological substitutes invented. The high levels of energy consumption characteristic of advanced societies cannot be sustained indefinitely and can never be possible on a global basis if fossil fuels are the only source. Even the current uranium-fueled nuclear reactors and the promised breeder reactors—themselves a source of increasing societal concern—would provide only a breathing space. Nuclear fusion and solar power, the "ultimate" solutions, are perhaps generations from reality. The profligate squandering of energy and minerals has fouled the environment in which we and future generations must live, and the exploitation of low-grade reserves that must inevitably follow will produce proportionately greater spoilage of the atmosphere and the landscape, will demand even greater energy outlays for extraction and refining, and can be realized only by committing an appalling proportion of world supplies of fresh water.

Technology's appetite for energy, materials, capital, and labor is the driving force of world interdependence as well as the source of much of the societal and international tensions that tear at the fabric of modern life.

Global interdependence is a relative matter, affecting different nations in differing ways and reinforced or offset to varying degrees by differences in national resources and national policies. It is necessary here to distinguish between sensitivity and vulnerability.* The long lines at U.S. gas stations in 1973 demonstrated our *sensitivity* to dependence on Arab oil. Our political *vulnerability* to this dependence, however, was limited by the fact that, in that year, 85 percent of our fuel consumption was from domestic sources. Japan, in contrast almost totally reliant on imported fuels, was both highly sensitive and extremely vulnerable to the Arab embargo.

Sensitivity can lead to painful economic dislocations, but these can often be avoided, or in any event ameliorated, by appropriate policy measures. Vulnerability is a different matter; it implies im-

---

*The distinction between *sensitivity* and *vulnerability* has been usefully and carefully employed by others (e.g., Joseph S. Nye, Jr., Independence and Interdependence, *Foreign Policy*, Spring 1976, 138 ff.) in theoretical analysis of such matters as mineral dependence.

pacts so basic to the structure and functioning of a national economy as to be beyond the reach of feasible domestic policy measures. In the worst case vulnerability can mean that a nation's policies become hostage in important respects to those of another nation, or group of nations, on whom it is reliant for a critical resource. The distinction between sensitivity and vulnerability adopted here applies to direct effects. The effects of the oil embargo on Japan and Western Europe, which produced intense strains in our own political and security alliances that have persisted in large measure, were a demonstration of our *indirect* vulnerability to this resource weapon.

Interdependence as often means sensitivity to the price of an imported commodity as vulnerability to political manipulation of its availability. Analyses confined to the economic dimensions of global interdependence lead to an imperfect perception, however. Interdependence has implications for national security, of course. It has more subtle sociological dimensions as well. While the world is far from a vast village, technological advances in communications and the large-scale interpersonal contacts that accompany our increased global movement have sensitized a majority of the world's population—and all of its political leadership—to global disparities in the quality of people's lives. Even the most dedicated nationalists or most impervious isolationists cannot close their eyes and ears, or their political perceptions, to the insistent demands for human equity that these disparities convey.

Governments use technology in performing their operational functions: building highways and airports, putting out fires, maintaining order, delivering mail, providing education, and so on. Most conspicuously, governments employ technology as the principal ingredient of their military strength.

Governments seek to encourage technological innovation in the service of national purposes. They support research and development (R&D) from public funds, not only to obtain those technological goods that are needed to perform the various roles of government itself but to insure an adequate technological base for private sector activities important to the national interest. In the United States the Department of Agriculture has, for a century, performed or funded nearly all the R&D that underlies our enormously productive agricultural economy. For fifty years the National Aeronautics and Space Administration (NASA) and its predecessor institutions have provided a large share of the technology that goes into the design of airplanes. The Atomic Energy Commission, later the Energy Research and Development Administration (ERDA), and now the Department of Energy, have spent billions of dollars in the last quarter century on the development and demonstration of nuclear power. A dozen other federal agencies also support civil R&D, but the direct support of R&D is only one—and possibly one of the less important—of the ways the government encourages technological innovation. Tax benefits, export sales assistance, the education of scientists and engineers and the countless varieties of subprofessionals required by the technological enterprise, the use of government procurement as an inducement; all these and more are important parts of governmental support to technological activity.

Increasingly, governments also influence the ways technology is used by the private sector, in the name of public health and safety but also as insurance that its benefits are not monopolized by a few at the expense of many. Intricate legal and administrative structures have grown up to guarantee (inadequately, perhaps) the purity of foods and the efficacy of drugs, to control environmental pollution and the exploitation of natural resources, to grant patents, to license specific uses of radio frequencies, to limit the export of technological goods when national security might be adversely affected, to set product standards, and on and on.

As domestic and international issues arising from the uses of technology and national and international policies for dealing with these are inextricably interrelated, so also is the reality of global technological interdependence among nations. The success of important domestic policies—regarding economic growth, for instance —depends on the acquiescence if not the active cooperation of international interests and other sovereignties. The pursuit of a stable and acceptable international political environment necessarily involves domestic compromises as well as international collective efforts to maximize the mutual benefits of cooperation, to set acceptable bounds on international competition, and to contain and resolve the confrontations these activities, and the related industrial and commercial activities, can provoke.

Interdependence implies cooperation, not in the service of higher principle but out of harsh necessity. However, interdependence is innately competitive as well; it is sustained by the ceaseless striking of new bargains. Too often the bargaining process breaks down over differing views of what is fair or even what is necessary. But interdependence means that the essential bargaining must be concluded; it can't be avoided or indefinitely postponed. Compromises are made. No one feels altogether happy with a compromise; a good compromise, often, is one with which all parties are equally unhappy. The realization of the fact of interdependence thus nourishes the seeds of rebellion against it until they blossom into the poisonous flower of confrontation.

Confrontation over issues stimulated by technological advance is a pervasive feature of foreign relations in an interdependent world. Illustrations abound: the nuclear arms race and the corollary issues of nuclear proliferation, verification, safeguarding of nuclear materials and installations, and the rest; the confrontations between the advanced industrial countries and the less developed countries over the goals and means of economic development and the proper sharing of the benefits of industrial technology between those who have evolved it and those whose mines, oil wells, and plantations sustain it; the debate about population growth and its demands on the diffusion of technology.

Technological developments have provoked international debates about infringements of national sovereignty: the potential impact of "open dissemination" policies for Landsat (Earth Resources Survey Satellite) data on national control of the exploitation of natural resources; the perceived conflict between freedom of oceanographic research and a nation's right to control the economic exploitation of its coastal waters; the complex and emotional issues surrounding the operations of technology-based multinational firms.

The very nature of technological impact is itself a confrontation between the old and the new, between stability and change. New ideas, new processes, new products, and the merchandising that stimulates a previously unappreciated need to own or consume them; all these challenge the old ways—the patterns of family and community life, the traditional values, the reach and the influence of established authority that are the basic fabric of national identity and, far more than the course of rivers or the chance location of mountain ranges, define the nation itself. The reach of modern communications and the urge for "progress" and the appetite for "modern" living that it stimulates defy the authority of governments everywhere.

Many of the benefits and problems brought by technology are beyond the reach of the authority of individual governments. Mutuality of self-interests thus creates powerful incentives for governments to organize collectively to promote the benefits and contain the risks. The United States currently belongs to at least thirty-four international, intergovernmental organizations (IOs) concerned specifically with technology or with public needs and concerns principally driven by technological development. The concerns of these IOs, taken together, are very broad: weather forecasting, aircraft navigation, contagious disease, marine pollution, regulation of deep-water fishing, restoration and maintenance of great cultural monuments, to cite a few examples. The political arrangements involved are always complex, and attempts to deal with many important issues continually break down in confrontations over conflicting values and priorities and, increasingly, through deep political cleavages related only indirectly, if at all, to the issues at hand. Concerted international decision making unavoidably entails some surrender of national sovereignty by each participant and thereby challenges deeply embedded mores. No nation can deny or avoid the necessity of international action, however, so the often painful efforts must go on.

The conduct of U.S. international relations goes far beyond the activities of the President or the Secretary of State. In the U.S. government, for example, the Department of Commerce controls exports, establishes product standards, promotes overseas sales by private firms; the Department of Defense provides training and advisory assistance to dozens of nations and gives or sells them much of their weaponry; the Department of the Treasury imposes and collects duties on imports and taxes on income derived from overseas operations; the Department of Agriculture sets quotas on imports and exports of foods and other farm products; the Department of Justice monitors the business practices of U.S. and foreign firms whose activities affect our suppliers and our markets; and every technical agency of government is involved in cooperative projects with foreign scientists and engineers. The list could be expanded almost indefinitely.

It is not only government that is involved in international relations. So are bankers, educators, students, shippers, air crews, and ordinary citizens who increasingly roam the world as tourists or entertain foreign visitors in their home communities. The most pervasive and, in terms of conspicuous impact, the biggest segment of the U.S. foreign affairs community, however, is industry. More than three-quarters of U.S. industrial consumption of ten of its most important raw materials is supplied by foreign nations. One-fourth or more of all U.S.–produced aircraft, computers, machinery, and scientific instruments are sold to foreign buyers. Literally thousands of U.S. industrial firms have established overseas subsidiaries to manufacture, sell, and service U.S.–designed products in foreign markets; some of the largest U.S. firms have established such subsidiaries in fifty or more foreign nations. Collectively, U.S. firms earned more than $18 billion from their overseas activities in 1975.

Government policy makers and industry managers perceive the

problems of international relations from different perspectives and judge the consequences of global technological activity in terms of different goals and notions of cost and value. These differences are often profound. National interests presumably subsume the totality of U.S. corporate interests, or at least all those morally defensible, but a nation's interests are not defined by simply adding up the interests of all of its constituencies. Interests are often in conflict, and assessing the impact of particular public policies involves measuring a benefit to one interest against a cost to others. (In mathematical terms, interests are not quantifiable, and the significant variables are incommensurable.) Small wonder, then, that national and international policy making for technology is so often described as a morass.

Most of the opportunities and issues that link technology to international relations have political and economic as well as technological dimensions. National and international efforts to deal with them usually proceed, fitfully and simultaneously, in each of these dimensions. Traditionally, and perhaps unavoidably, these various aspects are dealt with in different forums; national interests are advanced or defended by different spokesmen, often unaware of (or at least unappreciative of) the posture of their counterparts in other forums and negotiating frameworks. A better dialogue, at both national and international levels, among the participants in political, economic, and technological debates on major questions is essential to the public interest.

Public policy making is a judgmental process, reflecting implicit as well as explicit perceptions of appropriate goals and values. Government officials and politicians on the one hand and industrialists, businessmen, and technologists on the other view the need and purpose for government policy and the wisdom and workability of particular policy options from different points of view. Individuals and public interest groups who look at public policy making from the outside, so to speak, will often find fault with the perspectives of both government and industry. The challenge is to develop policy options that are technologically, politically, and economically sound. If that can be accomplished, the choice among them can be properly and safely left to the working of the political process. To develop sound policy options in these areas requires that the participants be adequately informed not only of the external political, economic, and technological realities that constrain the options but also of the goals and value systems of all those who are affected by the ultimate policy choice. Providing one perspective on such issues is a major goal of the pages that follow.

1

THE NATURE
OF TECHNOLOGY

As a first step to understanding the complex relationship between industry and government and between national and international policies in technology-related affairs, it is necessary to pin down some widely and loosely used concepts: What is meant by technology? How does it differ from science? We need also to ask why governments and industries invest in technology, what is the nature of the technological enterprise, and what this implies for public policy goals. These questions are addressed in this chapter.

WHAT ARE SCIENCE AND TECHNOLOGY?

The term *science* refers to a body of verifiable knowledge and an associated conceptual framework that attempts to structure the observable features of the natural world and to predict the outcome of observations and experiments yet to be conducted. The intellectual corpus of science evolves continuously in response to new data and to new theory. The driving forces of science are largely intellectual: curiosity, skepticism, and the search for order. But science also responds to social forces—the pursuit of prestige, the availability of public funds, the insatiable appetite for the new and the different.

Science is a cultural and aesthetic phenomenon, the product of an intellectual tradition, but much more as well. Of particular relevance here is that the modern-day training of engineers—the principal practitioners of technology—is deeply grounded in science. It is science that shapes their intellectual perspective insofar as their professional work is concerned. Their "mind-set" is scientific.

Technology, by contrast, is action-directed, concerned with doing things, solving practical problems, the creation of goods and services that are marketable, in the commercial sense or in the sense that they fill the perceived needs of nations as a whole. The values of technology, then, are both internal, in that good technology usually derives from good science, and external, in that they are derived from the worth society places on the applications of technology. In today's world technology draws heavily on science at the same time that it serves science (by providing new instruments and the like); in fact, it is relative success in nurturing and exploiting this symbiosis that characterizes the technologically advanced industries and nations. It was not always this way; a host of successful technologies predate the beginnings of science. Animals were domesticated, vessels plied the streams and oceans, windmills pumped water, clocks marked the passage of time, long before the scientific principles which—in the modern view—dictate the direction of progress in these matters were ever elucidated.

EMBODIMENTS OF TECHNOLOGY

Policy discussions about technology lay great stress on the matter of *embodiment*. Technology is most conspicuously embodied in things: products, components, hardware. New products that serve a unique function or displace traditional items with improvements in performance, reliability, costs, and style account for much of the economic and social importance of modern technology. Technology is also embodied in processed materials: plastics, special alloys, chemicals, synthetic fibers, and the like. Technology can be embodied in "software" as well; not only in the computer programs to which that jargon customarily refers but also in technical reports, manufacturing drawings and process specifications, design formulas, and the complex systems (e.g., the telephone services) that shape so much of modern society. Innovations in production processes—printed electronic circuits, numerically controlled machine tools, continuous extrusion of complex shapes in metal and plastic, freeze drying—help to maintain low selling costs for manufactured goods in the face of rising labor and materials costs. They also permit design approaches and performance qualities that would not otherwise be feasible. Process innovations account for the economies of scale—the "learning curves"—that are a major economic factor in the market successes of modern technological products. It is the rapid pace of the introduction of new production technologies (along with the high costs of product R&D and of market introduction) that gives high-technology industry its capital-intensive character.

Most important, technology is embodied in the skills and know-how of scientists, engineers, production and marketing supervisors, and laboratory and service technicians—technology "on the hoof," in a popular metaphor. Technology is and will remain far more than applied science. Technology involves a vast array of know-how: methods for working all forms of material; processes for leaching, etching, extracting, joining, coating, packaging, and so on; design procedures for creating complex systems and assemblages and the procedures for testing, maintaining, and operating them; the panoply of managerial skills essential to high-technology enterprise; the analytical methods, creative insights, and innovative approaches entailed in specifying a problem and the constraints to which a successful solution must conform. This list is by no means exhaustive. Failure to appreciate the multiple dimensions of the problems associated with successful introduction, production, and use of new, innovative applications of technology has been a major reason for the generally ineffectual and frustrating official international dialogue on technology policy. Whether the topic is mutual security, trade and investment, or development assistance, the simplistic notion that "technology transfer" is a straightforward, easily accomplished process that occurs with complete success or does not occur at all, depending solely on government decisions or the reverse transfer of a readily agreed sum of money, has made mockery of many well-intentioned public policies and international agreements. In succeeding chapters we will see how these embodiments are variously treated in such important policy domains as export control, foreign investment, technological assistance, and the institutional structuring of national and international organizations.

It is often said that technology per se—*naked* or disembodied technology—is of no societal significance, since only the ultimate uses of technology create social goods or disbenefits. This is analogous to the thesis in economic theory that money has no value in itself—a proposition that strikes people who have overdrawn their checking accounts as very academic and probably evidence of the naiveté of economists. Disembodied technology does have its own values for society, just as money does. One example of disembodied technology is a patent, a limited monopoly that seeks to balance incentives for inventors with the widest possible distribution of the benefits of innovation. The value of some (but by no means all) patents is attested by the vast amount of policy and legal attention given to them, nationally and internationally. Naked technology often takes on a kind of symbolic embodiment of great importance to international relations. The amount of technology a nation generates or controls is almost universally accepted as an important measure of that nation's relative place in the international scheme of things, whether measured in economic or military terms or in the more subjective areas of prestige or quality of life. Symbolic embodiment of technology, in this sense, is at most a surrogate for the social goods the exploitation of that technology could provide. It is, nonetheless, the subject of a great deal of political rhetoric in national and international forums alike. As the subsequent chapters will attempt to demonstrate, however, such symbolic embodiments—the substitution of an input measure for an output measure, the confusion of promise with achievement—can lead to policy conceptions that are ineffectual or even antiproductive.

R&D AND INNOVATION

Confusion about the complexities of the skills and processes involved in bringing a technological innovation successfully to the marketplace is not the only area where the dialogue among public officials suffers from lack of grounding in reality. Another, and very important, area of confusion is the nature and relationship of research and development and their place in the innovative process.

Research and development is a general rubric for a very wide spectrum of activities customarily divided among a variety of practitioners and a variety of institutions. R&D covers a range of activity that extends from the most basic "thought experiments" of mathematicians to the laboratory construction of prototypes of new products and systems. Within this spectrum lie *basic research* (undirected theoretical or experimental efforts to describe the behavior of the natural world), *applied research* (the use of the tools of basic research to obtain answers to specific questions about the behavior of certain forms or classes of natural things), and *advanced development* (the search for solutions to particular problems that stand in the way of achieving desired product or process performance). Such definitions are open to various interpretations, of course; the same activity may constitute basic research to the university professors (and their graduate students) who are performing it and applied research or even advanced development to the authorities, government or industrial, who are funding it. Where one stands depends on where one sits.

Whether basic or applied, research is inherently investigative in character; research seeks answers to questions. Development, on the other hand, seeks solutions to practical problems. Development is associated with the design of products, processes, and procedures to accomplish prescribed tasks that are perceived to have specific economic or social benefits.

Public officials, who seldom have had personal experience with the subtle, time-consuming, and expensive interplays of scientific, engineering, production, marketing, and managerial skills that characterize the technologically innovative process, frequently equate research with invention and R&D with successful introduction of technological innovation. Having authorized or appropriated money, they expect results. In reality, the public (or private) benefits of R&D are contingent. They occur when and if the results of the activity, embodied in goods and services, fulfill a public need. This is neither a reliably predictable or satisfactorily frequent outcome of the actual conduct of R&D. R&D must be understood as a risk venture; gambling (in the case of research) with the laws of nature and (in the case of development) with the whims of an uncertain marketplace.

The notion that "good" research produces useful invention is naive. Although invention can be, and sometimes is, a corollary of R&D, when it occurs, invention is accurately described as a fallout. R&D is not often undertaken with the deliberate objective of inventing something. Invention is a creative act, the result of a sudden insight or flash of genius. (This notion is deeply embedded in the premises of patent law.) However welcome such an occurrence would be in the context of an R&D effort, the rationale for R&D as a justifiable endeavor rests not on the expectation of the possibility of an invention but rather on the belief that logical plans, skillfully pursued and continuously adapted to new information and circumstances as they occur, will, with persistence, yield the intended result, whether that be a clearer vision of the secrets of nature or a potential solution to a practical problem. Invention, when it occurs, ends with the demonstration (which may be theoretical rather than experimental) that a wholly new mechanism or process will, in fact, function. Neither the inventor nor the patent-granting national authorities are expected to assume any responsibility for asserting or demonstrating the practicability of the invention or its potential viability in an economically competitive environment. Confusion between R&D and invention creates many problems in the international movement of industrial technology; these are addressed in Chapter 4.

When governments adopt policies for the encouragement of R&D and of invention, these activities are nearly always supported as surrogates for innovation. (Innovation, in this context, means the successful introduction to the marketplace of a new, technologically based product or process.) Innovation in the availability of public "goods" is the real goal of public policies for technology because, if it is successful in the marketplace, innovation creates jobs and tax revenue. Creating an environment that stimulates and nurtures successful technological innovation, then, is a major goal of governments.

Innovation, and not simply the continued efficient exploitation of mature technology, is critically important to economic growth. Data assembled by Richard Morse for the Secretary of Commerce's Technical Advisory Board[1] shows that young high-technology companies, whose principal products are in the early rapid-growth phase of the product life-cycle,[2] have typically demonstrated in recent years average annual growth (compounded) in sales and in new jobs created of about 40 percent. Major technologically based companies whose products typically lie at the peak of the product life-cycle—when the innovative impact has reached its maximum —show average annual growth rates in sales of 10 to 15 percent and in new jobs created of around 4 percent. Mature firms whose products customarily embody older, more familiar technologies exhibit average annual growth in sales in the same range as those of the major technologically based companies, but create new jobs at a much slower rate, 1 or 2 percent per year.

INDUSTRIAL STRATEGIES FOR R&D

As I pointed out earlier, R&D is a risk venture. Industrial management strategies must take this basic fact into account. Private management undertakes in its R&D planning to balance risks— technological, investment, and competitive risks—against the potential benefits of capturing (even if for a limited period) the dominance of a market sector that is promising in terms of present size, potential for growth, and profitability. The goal is to achieve a limited market monopoly. U.S. law recognizes and legitimizes this objective in the constitutional and legislative provisions dealing with patents, trade secrets, and proprietary know-how. Industrial strategies rely on all three.

A firm may choose a defensive strategy, investing its R&D budget in incremental improvements to a product or process that improves its profitability within its market niche. Alternatively, the firm can pursue more advanced technologies for narrower but more sophisticated, and accordingly less competitive, markets. Greater technological and market risks are involved, but profitability is higher, and the possibility of a breakthrough to market dominance is always there. For even the most technologically advanced firms, however, the advanced technology route has become less attractive or even unfeasible as a result of inflation. The high cost of money, combined with the long payout periods that generally accompany the introduction of a truly innovative product, has simply made the combination of costs and risks prohibitive for many firms.

The "defensive" strategy just referred to is not necessarily unsophisticated. One of the most striking features of modern industrial technology is its high rate of obsolescence. New innovations force out older products and processes because they offer cost savings or because they provide performance not previously available. Since industrial managers seek to maximize the return on invested capital and skill, they plan their R&D not only to provide innovations for new markets but also to influence the rate of obsolescence of their present product lines, by introducing incremental improvements and, when these no longer suffice, by making their own products obsolete in their own markets. This is why currently useful technology can't be sold or licensed to unaffiliated firms at a marginal cost. The price charged for technology provided to another firm depends not on its cost but on the importance of the market for the products of that technology accessible to the buying firm and inaccessible to the supplying firm. There are, in addition, situations where technology is sold to generate the funds needed to protect the originating firm's share of a more important market.

Multinational firms, with the advantages arising from their ability to aggregate a broad horizontal market and to take advantage of economies of labor and scale in production often denied to firms focused on a single market, characteristically employ a mixed strategy. Older, less sophisticated technologies for which the production problems and customer service requirements are thoroughly understood are moved out to subsidiaries in less demanding national markets, while the new, more advanced technologies displace them in the home markets.[3] This strategy has a dual advantage: It extends the profitable life of older designs for which the costs of R&D, tooling, market development, and so forth are already amortized, while making room for technological leadership (and for working out the inevitable "bugs" close to the centers of expertise) in the home market. Pursuit of this strategy tends to concentrate the R&D activity in the home country, a source of considerable complaint by the less advanced countries (see Chapter 6).

GOVERNMENT INVESTMENT IN TECHNOLOGY

The motivations of governmental investment in R&D are different from those of industry, and more complex. In general, governments invest in R&D when important public benefits are perceived but individual firms are unable to balance the business benefits of the innovation with the various costs and risks entailed. The primary applications of this principle are, for obvious reasons, in the military and space areas, though a similar motivation exists in such areas as health care and agricultural R&D. Government R&D investments also entail risks (that is perhaps the only rational justification for government intervention), but they are primarily the possibility that the technological objectives will not be achieved. The source of investment funds, for government, is not as directly dependent on returns from previous investments as is the case in private industry. Thus competitive risks may exist in principle, in the sense that international political competition is often implicit, but they are entirely different from private sector R&D risks. Furthermore, the penalties for failure, poor judgments or bad luck are clearly of a different order for government-supported R&D than for private R&D investment. History does not provide any examples of governments (let alone nations) that have fallen because of undertaking risks in science and technology, but the landscape is strewn with the remains of industrial enterprises caught short in this regard. In addition, government R&D risks in the United States are limited by the fact that procurement policy, in the case of contract-supported R&D, frequently requires (implicitly, if not explicitly) that the R&D contractor bear a share of the cost and risk.

Government expenditures for R&D are very large. In the United States these account for about 15 percent of the relatively controllable portion of the Federal budget.* In fiscal year 1976 federal funding for support of R&D exceeded $20 billion; industry's support of R&D from its own funds amounted to $16.6 billion. Of the total R&D performed, about 70 percent was in industry.[4]

It is easy for public officials to fall into the trap of assuming that the sum of the technology interests of all federal agencies is equal to the national interest. The marketplace sees this differently. For example, when *both* federal and corporate R&D expenditures in fiscal year 1974 are included, five U.S. industrial sectors account for more than 80 percent of total industrial R&D expenditures.[5] In rank order these are: electrical equipment and communications, aircraft and missiles, machinery (including computers), chemicals and allied products, and motor vehicles. The first two sectors each account for one-fourth of the national total and the other three for something over 10 percent each. If only company-financed R&D is considered, the same sectors account for about 75 percent of the national total, but the disparities among the sectors are much smaller: For the chemical sector, 91 percent of its R&D is company-financed; for motor vehicles, 87 percent; for machinery and computers, 86 percent; for electrical equipment and communications, 53 percent; and for aircraft and missiles, only 22 percent.

There are important national differences in government funding of technology development. The scale of funding differs among countries not only in absolute terms but also as a proportion of gross national product (GNP). The most recent available data[6] show the U.S.S.R. devoting 3.1 percent of its GNP to research and development; West Germany, 2.4 percent; the United States, 2.2 percent; Japan, 1.9 percent; and France, 1.7 percent. Because of differences in definition and national accounting, these numbers are not truly comparable; however, the published data make clear the national differences in trends. R&D expenditures as a percentage of GNP have declined steadily for 10 years in the United States and for six years in France, while the other three countries cited have shown steady increases.

Important national differences occur also in the sectors emphasized in government R&D funding. In recent years the porportion of government R&D outlays devoted to national defense and space is about 70 percent for the United States, 46 percent for the United Kingdom, 36 percent for France, 23 percent for West Ger-

---

*To an increasing degree expansion of the federal budget is due to the rising costs of such "uncontrollable" items as Social Security, veterans' benefits, and interest on the federal debt.

many, and 2 or 3 percent for Japan. (Estimates for the U.S.S.R. are not available, but the figure probably lies above that for the United States.)

From these comparisons it is obvious that the impact of government R&D support on the production and marketing of goods for civil applications varies even more widely among our trading partners than between the United States and the U.S.S.R.

INTERNATIONAL DIFFUSION OF TECHNOLOGY

The high costs of introduction and absorption of important technological innovations increasingly demand markets larger than those afforded by individual countries (even the United States) or trade groupings (even the EC). The most successful technology-based firms have responded by identifying their markets in functional, rather than national, terms. The national-market strategy has proved limiting not only in market size but also in its tendency to demand a breadth of product line that is in itself uneconomic, spreading R&D resources too thinly to achieve a leadership position in any product area.* Similar considerations have created pressures for specialization among high-technology firms.

The rapidity with which modern technology diffuses internationally increases the difficulty of public policy making in this area. Product-embodied technology diffuses first to the international marketplace as it finds application in the customers' operations or becomes incorporated in their products. However, it quickly begins to diffuse to competitive producers (who may also be consumers of the original innovation). The mechanisms for this diffusion process are many. Publication of relevant concepts and data in scientific and technical journals and books, when not restricted by the proprietary policies of the innovating firm or by military classification, is an important medium. The public disclosure of technical principles and concepts that is inherent in patents is a significant vehicle for international diffusion of technology. The licensing of foreign manufacturers (including the affiliates of multinational firms) to use an innovation in their own operations, is, of course, a deliberate effort to

---

*The performance of the European aircraft and computer industries in the 1960s provides a compelling illustration of the point (see Robert H. Hayes, Europe's Computer Industry: Closer to the Brink. *Columbia Journal of World Business*, Summer 1974, 113–122).

transfer technology abroad. Technological diffusion is an unavoidable corollary of producing and marketing a product in most instances. Subcontracting the manufacture of special parts and subassemblies diffuses the technology involved; so does the process of application engineering—that is, the specialized technical assistance provided by manufacturers to their customers in order to facilitate the customers' successful utilization of the innovative product.

It is important to recognize that significant technological innovations fill some perceived or latent public need. That is the whole purpose of the innovative effort. Considering that fundamental, and keeping in mind the tremendous scale of R&D outlays in all industrialized countries, it is not surprising that an important innovation (or a number of different innovations responding in roughly equivalent ways to the same need) will emerge more or less simultaneously from different laboratories and in different countries. The very knowledge that someone, somewhere, has succeeded in solving an important problem, even accompanied by only the sketchiest details of the form the successful innovation takes, is frequently all that is needed to prompt a competitive innovation elsewhere within a short time and without any specific transfer of technology. Knowing that a technological solution is possible is a powerful stimulus to the innovative efforts of others, and permits them to abandon their own efforts intended to prove that a solution is impossible (a by no means insignificant part of organized R&D) and to focus R&D efforts on the approach known or suspected to be employed by those responsible for the original success.

The international diffusion of an important technology cannot be prevented; at least so far efforts to do so have always failed. It is possible to delay the process, but usually at the expense of market growth. It may be possible to deliberately structure and control the process of diffusion in support of some national or corporate objective. Preventing diffusion, however, appears, at a minimum, to require the innovating enterprise and nation to forgo the full benefits of the innovation and probably requires the imposition of other measures that will ultimately damage and weaken the capacity for innovation in the industry or nation that adopts such a strategy.

Though international diffusion of technology appears inevitable, there are formidable barriers to the process, even in those circumstances where the transfer is the deliberate goal of both parties. Before we leave the topic, it will be useful to touch on the most important of these.

First, there are economic barriers. Differences in structure among national economies are reflected in national differences among industrial firms, even in the same sector. These differences may pose difficulties in financing the purchase or licensing of foreign technologies and the investments necessary to bring an imported technology to fruition in the local market. National differences in market size or market preferences may pose barriers to the use of imported technology. Differences in industrial infrastructure may make it difficult or impossible to obtain, in a foreign country, specialized materials or services that were critical to the success of a particular technology in the originating nation.

Cultural differences between nations can also pose significant obstacles to the international transfer of technology. This is obvious in the area of market preferences. What may not be so obvious is the importance of this factor to the ability of a firm to manufacture an innovative product, or to exploit an innovative production process, developed in another country. Language itself can be a barrier, even among nations ostensibly sharing a common one. Particular technical terms (jargon) in one country often convey quite a different meaning to natives of another country. Labor practices are different among nations, and skills taken for granted when production drawings and process specifications are prepared may be found in some quite different labor category, or not at all, in another country. Differing standards of workmanship and differing standards for commonly used hardware items (nuts, bolts, wire, solder, adhesives, paint, etc.) can prove to be major obstacles to the successful transfer of a technological innovation. The important point is that all these matters, being a part of the underlying culture of a nation, are seldom (if at all) taken into account in the production documentation or the description of design approaches. They are taken for granted and thus often prove most difficult to identify and overcome—being taken for granted, they don't intrude on the consciousness of the people involved on either end of the transfer process.

Technology impacts on the way we live—that is its purpose. These impacts, on societies as well as on individuals and on global interdependence, lead to a wide range of public policies, implicit as well as explicit and international as well as domestic. Such policies are intended to shape the exploitation of technology to public needs and to reserve, insofar as is possible and desirable, its principal benefits to the innovating nation. Chapter 2 explores the range of these impacts on public needs and interests and the conflicts that invariably arise.

Notes

1. Morse, Richard S. Innovative Technology: What Is Its Impact on the U.S. Economy? *Professional Engineer,* August 1976.

2. Vernon, Raymond. International Investment and International Trade in the Product Cycle. *Quarterly Journal of Economics,* 1966, **80,** 190–207.

3. Nabseth, L., and Ray, G.F., eds. *The Diffusion of New Industrial Processes.* London: Cambridge University Press, 1974.

4. *National Patterns of R&D Resources: Funds and Manpower in the United States–1953–1976.* Washington, D.C.: National Science Foundation, 1976.

5. Research and Development in Industry—1974. Washington, D.C.: National Science Foundation, 1976.

6. Science Indicators—1974. Washington, D.C.: National Science Board, 1976.

2

PUBLIC POLICY AND
THE POLITICAL PROCESS

Governmental response to the many issues created by technological progress is most often exemplified by the variety of formulations, positions, and rules for behavior that fall under the rubric of public policy. In the following chapter we will look at three areas of public policy of particular relevance to our subject: science policy, technology policy, and foreign policy. First, however, it is useful to examine briefly the general nature of public policy—what it is, how it fits into the structure of the political process, and how public policies are made (or identified).

A DEFINITION OF PUBLIC POLICY

Policy making is an attempt to perfect institutional behavior. A policy is an established principle or practice for dealing with a particular class of issues that recur from time to time. It implies a conscious choice by a level of authority (legislative or executive) competent to act in such matters; a choice that, once made, provides guidance not only for those who will carry out the day-by-day implementation but also for those, at home and abroad, who seek to understand national intentions and priorities. The articulation of policy is an attempt to structure the political agenda.

Policy, by its nature, presumes a degree of stability in the character of political issues and events and in those perceptions of public goals and priorities that determine a government's response to them. Government seeks to reinforce that stability by imposing a particular discipline on its bureaucracy and on the broader political arena.

THE GENESIS OF POLICY

Whether public policy is articulated in legislation or in the directives of the executive branch, its genesis most often lies in the political importance of a particular public interest; cleaning up the environment, for example, or maximizing competition among private suppliers of various goods. There is usually widespread, if sometimes latent, support for political action on such matters. Particular policies are always resisted, of course, by those who perceive the costs to their special interests as disproportionate to the benefits to them, but in the domestic arena the principle of the greater good is considered served if the policy chosen has the support of a majority of the elected representatives of the people (or two-thirds of them, if the White House should disagree with the Congress on which goods are, in a particular instance, the greater ones.)

Standing alone, a public policy derived in this fashion may serve its intended purpose very well, so long as the circumstances relevant to the issues do not evolve in directions that vitiate its intended effect. But circumstances do change, and public policies do not stand alone. Dramatic changes in the international market for petroleum put in question long-standing domestic energy policies, for example. Economic policies may conflict with environmental protection policies; tax and regulatory policies can operate to limit the public benefits from technological innovation. As these examples indicate, individual public policies serving particular public interests may impact adversely on other, equally important, public interests. When this is the case, the political system is expected to act to resolve or eliminate the conflict, so that the broader public interest is optimally served.

Political adjustment to problems arising from conflicts among particular public policies or from the unintended side effects of a particular policy is not easily accomplished. Vested interests are aroused and jurisdictional disputes surface among those who seek to define policy and among those whose bureaucratic status rests on an unchallenged right to interpret policy in a specific area. These various conflicts may remain unresolved until political imperatives force direct intervention by the White House or the Congressional leadership.

CONFLICTS IN POLICY MAKING

When quite different value systems and conceptual frameworks come together in a decision-making situation—as is usually the case when technology and foreign policy impinge on each other—good decisions are particularly difficult to achieve. The various partisans often lack a common understanding of all the factors involved; they are unable to "stipulate the facts." The most relevant value perceptions are often incommensurable; there is no way to measure objectively the net balance between benefits in one area and disbenefits in another. Rank ordering of the choices becomes a frustrating and often contentious process, usually requiring the kind of compromise that makes everyone unhappy. Because so few officials have the authority to commit all of the disparate resources involved in such choices (or the self-confidence to accept responsibility for the disbenefits involved), a final decision often involves the highest levels of government, a situation which further exacerbates the frustration of the experts on all sides.

The chief executive can always, in principle, resolve conflicts of purpose and authority among officials in the administration. Dealing with the authorities arising from bureaucratic expertise and working involvement with the issues is much harder. One reason is the inevitable existence of the "back channel," that is, the peer relationships among the experts in various parts of the bureaucracy and with their counterparts outside government (and perhaps influential in the political party not currently in power). For most bureaucrats in private enterprise as well as in government, the professional recognition essential to self-esteem and job advancement is conferred by the peer group not by elected or appointed officials. The latter come and go, but the peer group is a constant. In no public policy area does this fact have greater influence than in technology policy. Elected officials rarely possess any substantive expertise in science and technology matters themselves. If the views of a bureaucratic underling are contrary to those of an official, or if they claim a scientific basis (especially if they are supported by outside scientists or technical specialists), it becomes difficult if not impossible for the responsible official to fully exercise policy-making prerogatives.

THE DYNAMICS OF POLICY MAKING

Public policy can be expressed in a variety of ways. Policy can be expressed in law or in binding international treaties that have the force of law. More frequently, perhaps, public policy is given expression in "sense of the Congress" resolutions or in analogous pronouncements by the President. The latter frequently employ rhetoric that appears to impute a degree of unalterability that, in the final analysis, is spurious. Such phrases as *irrevocable commitment* and *absolute guarantee* or pledges of *full support* are intended to elevate the political visibility of the policy articulated—which often succeeds—and also to give an impression of permanence that no public offical in a democracy like ours, certainly, is, in fact, in a position to assure. In reality, of course, both the circumstances that shape policy and the governments that state policy change, and policies will inevitably change also.

Policies expressed in terms of long-term guarantees face an unavoidable problem of credibility. This is especially true in matters of foreign policy, where the government that changes its mind is beyond the reach of political retribution. Presidential guarantees are particularly suspect because, as foreign officials know as well as anybody, Congress can make them empty.

Policies expressed in negative terms, that is, those that threaten withdrawal of benefits previously available, are more credible in the international arena, since the power of either the Congress or the president (or, for that matter, lesser officials) to cut off the flow of support is undeniable and amply illustrated in history.

The ways in which public policy is made are various. Policy is frequently made by inaction. This is particularly important because inaction on a policy issue creates an environment in which aberrant decisions and actions thrive. Inaction can lead to a worse situation than if the wrong policy were publicly adopted, simply because the latter situation is usually more visible and hence easier to correct.

Public policy is often made by a trade-off procedure that reaches its natural conclusion when dissatisfaction is distributed among advocates of the contending interests in inverse proportion to their political clout. Policy can be made by defining specific objectives, establishing relative priorities, allocating fiscal and human resources, or creating new institutional structures or dismantling existing ones. Most important policy decisions, however embodied, have the effect of changing the allocation of authority among officials. Little wonder that government officials see policy making as their highest duty.

PUBLIC INVOLVEMENT IN
POLICY MAKING

As in most aspects of public policy formulation, the public has as-sumed an increasingly active and influential role in the formulation of technology policy. The history of nuclear energy is a good illustra-tion. The basic policy decision to put the resources of the federal government behind the development and demonstration of atomic power was formulated in the Atomic Energy Commission (AEC) and endorsed by President Eisenhower. Initially the Congressional policy-making role in this area was largely confined to appropriating the necessary funds. As public interest grew—largely as a result of AEC publicity—so did that of the Congress. A Joint Committee on Atomic Energy was created to provide oversight, and individual members became very active in proposing and developing support for specific programs. However, critics of the policy in and out of Congress were becoming more vocal, and their concerns became the rallying point for increasing numbers of the public. A breakthrough came with passage of the National Environmental Policy Act of 1969, providing, among other things, that environmental impact state-ments for proposed nuclear plants be prepared and made public. Very quickly public groups opposed to the development of nuclear power discovered in the process of judicial review of such state-ments the means to force attention to public concerns and even to establish specific policy constraints on particular projects. The democratization of the policy-making process in the nuclear power field did not stop there. State legislatures and even municipal au-thorities, under public pressure, began to establish policies govern-ing the location and operations of nuclear power plants, often in contradiction to avowed federal policy. Perhaps the ultimate in pub-lic participation was reached in the elections of 1976, when public referenda on nuclear power policy appeared on the ballots of six states.

The evolution of policy making in a highly technical area from the private deliberations of executive branch experts to, ultimately, the public referendum process is a major development with profound implications. In considering this development it is important to rec-ognize that public influence on government policy making operates rather differently from public participation in national elections. The notion of a more or less homogeneous collective body of voters, characterized by a continuum of opinions and interests on the one hand and of motivation for active participation on the other, may be relevant to the national elective process (and even to the development of the statistical sampling schemes on which forecasts of elections are based), but it does not usefully illuminate the realities of public influence on policy making by government officials. In this context, the public functions as a large number of relatively discrete constituencies that frequently overlap (professional associations, trade unions, industrial associations, environmental action groups, etc.).

Politically motivated individuals concerned with a particular public policy issue customarily act by associating themselves with the various constituencies they connect most directly with their interests. Having done so, they grant the accepted leadership of each of those constituencies their proxy.

In the area of science and technology policy, the situation just described is very much at work. Individuals concerned with these matters usually (but not always) are content to have their views on policy matters conveyed to governmental officials through such surrogates as the leadership of the academic scientific community (who, in the nature of things, are largely self-appointed), through professional engineering and scientific societies and the National Academies of Science and Engineering, through various trade and industrial associations, through environmental and consumer action groups, through the various armed forces associations, and so on. The views on public policy that emerge are obviously selective, in that they reflect only a limited mutuality of the values and interests of the members of each group, and they may be distorted by the understandable propensity of the public representatives of each group to express positions in a rhetoric more forceful and with a greater militancy than most individual members of the group would employ. (In fact, these attributes are among the most important that influence the selection of leaders by such groups.)

The virtues of participatory democracy are dear to the American political ethic, and it is right that this be so. At the same time public officials and conscientious citizens should be constantly aware of the potential for conflict and for distortion of the intent of constitutional government that lie in the implicit conflict between participatory democracy on the one hand and representative democracy on the other. Our Constitution rests, ultimately, on its embodiment of the principle of equity. All are presumed to be provided a fair share of the "public voice," and "one man, one vote" is the procedural strategem by which responsible government is to insure representation for all those governed. The influence of special interest groups in the formulation of public policy, which is seen by some as enshrining the notion of participatory democracy, has the potential effect of giving any individual who wishes to take advantage of it the opportunity to cast as many "votes" as he pleases, limited only by the number of such groups seeking to influence public policy in the direction of his biases.

The last decade or so has been a period in which the mechanisms available to special interest groups have proliferated and also have become more effective. Public interest groups, supported in many instances by very able legal talents, have availed themselves of the mechanism of Congressional hearings and the accessibility of a responsive press to advance their particular interests. The environmental movement has had remarkable success in achieving legislative recognition of environmental concerns and has learned to employ judicial means to press its interests with awesome effectiveness, particularly through the strategy of challenging the adequacy of environmental impact statements prepared by federal agencies and private utilities for a wide variety of important programs.[1] Though some of these activities might be questioned in terms of the larger public interest, the general trend is undoubtedly good. New legislation, such as the Freedom of Information Act of 1974 and the Advisory Committee Act of 1972, has created opportunities with enormous implications for future public participation in governmental policy making. The total impact on public science and technology policy formulation of these and comparable developments is already profound.

One special aspect of public involvement in science policy merits specific mention. Those federal agencies now responsible for the majority of public support for basic research—the National Institutes of Health and the National Science Foundation—rely heavily on "peer review" in their selection of research proposals for grant support. In the peer-review process nongovernmental scientists expert in the pertinent area of research are asked to rate research proposals in terms of their scientific quality and relevance to research priorities. It is apparent that the resulting judgments will be strongly influenced by the review panel's knowledge of the work of the individual scientist making the proposal and by collective (though perhaps unspoken, and even unconscious) perceptions of scientific priorities. For just these reasons the peer-review system is under nearly continuous attack by those members of the research community who perceive it as rewarding past performance instead of opening up new opportunities and by nonscientist government officials who believe that the results do not adequately reflect public priorities. While it is hard to visualize a system that would insure a higher quality level for grant-supported research, there is no doubt that, in general, peer review tends to perpetuate the prevailing views of science. Such a self-reinforcing system inevitably has difficulty understanding and responding to external pressures, particularly from the world outside the United States.

Note

1. Hill, Gladwin. Environmental Impact Statements, Practically a Revolution. *New York Times*, December 5, 1976.

3

FOREIGN POLICY, SCIENCE POLICY AND TECHNOLOGY POLICY

FOREIGN POLICY

Global interdependence and its intrusion into areas of great public interest have enormous implications for the shaping of foreign policy and the conduct of foreign relations. Interdependence blurs the distinction between foreign policy and domestic policy; no longer does politics stop at the nation's borders. One effect is a startling proliferation in the number of government agencies formally engaged in international relations. Another effect, discussed in Chapter 9, is the increasing importance of international organizations to foreign policy. The nature of power is changing irreversibly—the power of a nation is no longer determined solely by the size of its military establishment and the strength of its currency in international exchange, and the primacy of the President and the Secretary of State in U.S. foreign policy no longer remains unchallenged; indeed it cannot. Too many domestic constituencies are affected by international relations in an interdependent world to expect that the President and the senior secretary can maintain foreign policy as a royal domain. That domestic political constituencies should intrude into the domain of foreign policy is not only unavoidable but unassailable on practical and moral grounds. It does complicate things, not simply because the political expression of the interests of domestic constituencies is usually parochial, but because the realities of international interdependence affect these domestic constituencies unequally. For example, the failure of the Russian wheat harvest in 1975, coinciding as it did with severe food shortages in the least developed countries, provided an economic boon to U.S. wheat farmers but a painful rise in food prices for U.S. households. The well-publicized debate between the (then) Secretary of Agriculture and the (then) Secretary of State over U.S. grain export policy exemplified but a narrow aspect of the multidimensional nature of foreign policy debate in a pluralistic society confronting an interdependent world.

Science and technology both impinge greatly on foreign policy. Science per se is an intellectual discipline, aiming for a body of objective truth. Its premises and values have much of the character of an ideology, and its social impact ranks with that of other major ideologies in today's world. Science is unique in that it can and does coexist with other ideologies within nations and demands and receives a special loyalty from its practitioners that frequently transcends loyalties to political ideologies. In terms of international relations, cooperation in science serves transnational interests and can therefore serve as a bridge between influential groups in nations whose special interests and political ideologies otherwise appear incompatible.

Modern technology is a principal agent for social change. As such, and in light of its ubiquity and of public awareness of its accomplishments and shortcomings, it is a major influence in international relations and, inevitably, in foreign policy. Technology impinges on foreign policy in several significant ways:

- The availability of a viable technology can facilitate the accomplishment of particular foreign policy objectives, and the lack of the necessary technology can limit progress toward others. Examples abound: international telecommunications, flight safety, food assistance to the undernourished, arms control, pollution control in international waters and the atmosphere, and so forth.

- Measures to encourage or to limit the access of other nations to technology held by one nation lead to major political issues between trading partners, allies, and antagonists and between the industrialized and the less developed countries. Domestic constituencies who see their particular interests adversely affected by such measures often react noisily and sometimes decisively.

- The promise of preferred access to technology has, especially in recent years, been offered as a principal inducement to other nations to accept political postures or alignments advantageous to the technology-offering state.

- Technological advances are sometimes viewed as threatening the sovereignty of nations, as in the surveying of natural resources from space or direct broadcasting from satellites.

- Application of certain technologies can produce transborder effects, with a consequent need for internationally agreed restraints or guidelines, as in the area of weather modification.

- Certain technological goals of wide interest—space, uranium enrichment, health-care delivery, and the like—can serve as a basis for international collaborative efforts with important mutual benefits.

The "technological balance of power" is perceived by most national leaders, here and abroad, as a profound reality, and indeed it is. The ability to generate, trade for, or otherwise acquire advanced technologies seen as essential to national defense, economic growth (including a favorable international trade position), and the perceived needs and desires of citizens, and the ability to exploit this technology efficiently, is the identifying mark of a modern nation. However, the concept of the technological balance of power eludes precise definition and quantification. The famous "technological gaps" study by the Organization for Economic Co-operation and Development (OECD), undertaken in the late sixties,[1] failed to identify the disparities claimed by Servan-Schreiber[2] and others or even to agree on useful measures of relative technological strength. The reason is that technology is simply an input to the socioeconomic process, a poor surrogate for the output benefits that are the real concern.

Foreign Policy Imperatives

The quest for a viable foreign policy and the confrontation among foreign policies that are the business of diplomacy must proceed in the context of a number of international imperatives—that is, certain public interests that transcend national politics and can be effectively served only by global harmonization of national policies or by concerted international action. Technology can facilitate or limit the spectrum of feasible responses to these imperatives, surely including the following:

- Stability of the world order. Change is inevitable, and in many areas change is itself imperative. However, the international impacts of change on the internal political structure of nations or their international policies must not be so great or so damaging to other legitimate interests as to lead to an uncontrollable destabilization of world society.

- Constructive measures to stem and reverse the ever-widening gap between the rich nations and the poor nations. Access to essential food, energy sources, raw materials, and manufactured goods— even on concessional terms*—is a necessary but not sufficient condition for success. Also necessary are controls on population growth (or, as a minimum, workable incentives for reducing birth rates to levels commensurate with economic realities) and construction of international economic (trading, investment, etc.) relationships that can be sustained by a mutuality of perceived self-interests and yet reduce or contain economic and social disparities.

- Limiting potential military conflict. The costs and frequent unworkability of military intervention as a solution to political and economic conflict are increasingly apparent. The effects of a nuclear war are seen by most nations—whether or not they now possess or could acquire nuclear weapons—as more than apocalyptic; even the righteous would perish. Nonetheless, in the absence of credible alternative means for the containment and resolution of international conflict, one-fifth of all of the potentially economically productive people in the world are under arms. The United States and the U.S.S.R. together spend more on their military budgets than the entire world spends on public education and public health.[3] Unless we are to abandon all hope, the world community must, as a matter of highest priority, continue the search for viable alternatives for the resolution of international conflict.

- Recognizing and, through suitably directed technology, alleviating the undesirable side effects of the explosion of technology. The public demand that governments identify and adopt constructive measures to deal with the social costs of technology is a pressing international reality. National priorities in this regard differ in significant ways, and national means for dealing with these issues are proving inadequate in the face of the global nature of

---

Concessional terms, in this context, implies that, for humanitarian or at least political reasons, the richer trading partner offers prices, credit, or availability of essential goods on a more favorable basis than would be dictated by a free market.

the problems. International consensus on public interests and priorities, specific objectives, and the international institutional and financial arrangements necessary to deal with the problems is becoming increasingly urgent.

In the face of the many difficulties sketched above, it is obvious that effective international collaboration is required. No one would deny this, but everyone is frustrated by the apparent failure of international efforts to achieve, or even to demonstrate significant progress toward, these goals. In part, this situation is the result of expecting too much of technology and of international civil servants as experts on its proper use.

International Collaboration

Not all attempts at international collaboration toward a common purpose are failures. International postal and telecommunications services are very good and constantly improving, in the face of intense competition among national enterprises for dominance of the enormous markets for the technological products employed. International weather reporting and forecasting services routinely employ technologies very close to the state of the art in an area of public service of enormous economic significance. International exploitation of technology to improve maritime and aviation safety have been markedly successful, and international efforts toward conservation of wild species have made significant progress.

Nonetheless, success to date in many areas has been very limited. In arms control, for example, the greatest achievement of the nuclear superpowers has been simply to talk about the issues, in spite of the great value even limited agreement would have for both sides.

The frustrations associated with multilateral efforts to work out common understandings and cooperative actions in important matters has led many governments to focus their attention on more limited avenues of approach—bilateral or regional. Obviously, working with one's established allies or immediate neighbors offers the advantages of more clearly and credibly definable mutual interests, but it also has the disadvantage that agreements achieved in these narrower groupings may appear confrontational to uninvolved nations, who may be the most important influences in a major problem area.

Meaningful international collaboration, whether bilateral, regional, or global, is very difficult to accomplish. Nevertheless, the number of crucial problems that can be solved effectively in no other way is large and growing. The issue that must be recognized and dealt with is how to achieve this collaboration.

SCIENCE POLICY

National science policy has an important impact on the interactions between technology and foreign affairs. This is true in its own right—science per se plays a significant role in international relations—and also because science policy is often a surrogate domain for the debate and resolution of matters that in actuality are issues of technology policy.

Post-World War II

Science policy—defined as a policy for the public support of scientific enquiry, argued on the basis that scientific discovery contributes to the wealth and power of nations—had early beginnings, going back at least as far as the court of Czar Peter the Great at the beginning of the eighteenth century. Its historical development is a fascinating subject, but one beyond the scope of this book. The period of interest here began with World War II, when the scientific communities of Germany, Great Britain, the United States, and other nations came into intensive contact with government officials and impressed the latter greatly with their ability to convert arcane knowledge to the solution of practical problems. This experience convinced both scientists and politicians that there were great potentials for the pursuit of national goals in the development of a symbiotic relationship between the two communities. Unfortunately, the two groups identified the problem differently. Recognizing the importance of the scientific enterprise as a component of the national culture, the scientific community stressed public responsibility for its nurture. The politicians, on the other hand, recalling the wartime relationship, saw as the quid pro quo for support of the the scientific enterprise from the public treasury the solution of a variety of problems that were regarded by the public as important but that proved resistant to purely political solutions. Recognition by both sides of this crucial dichotomy of perceptions and expectations came slowly.

The common ground—agreement on the legitimacy of the demands of the scientific enterprise for a share of the public wealth—was the scene of remarkable progress. Beginning at the end of World War II at a very modest level, federal support of the U.S. R&D enterprise had, by 1968, reached an annual rate of $15 billion, nearly 10 percent of the total federal budget; 155,000 engineers and scientists were engaged in federally supported R&D. Only $2.4 billion of that total went to basic research (rather loosely defined), but this is no small sum, and the research enterprise and postgraduate enrollment in the universities grew very rapidly.

For governments management of the explosive growth of the R&D enterprise required institutional adjustments as well. By 1968 most industrialized countries had created ministers of science or a functionally equivalent post (in the United States a President's Science Advisor*), with more or less direct access to the head of state. It was presumed that this would insure a proper balance of support to the various sectors of science in the pursuit of generally recognized national objectives. In actuality, however, the overwhelming majority of public expenditures for R&D went to sectors that enjoyed both long-standing ties with the top levels of government and powerful constituencies of their own among legislators and in the private sector. By 1968 federal R&D obligations in the United States were allocated as follows:[4]

Defense (including atomic weapons)	52%
Space	28
Health	7
Energy	2
All other	11

Basic and applied research support accounted for 3 percent of the 1968 totals. The percentages cited overwhelmingly reflect development activity.

Understandably, those responsible for the management of mission-oriented R&D preferred to take the case for support directly to the Congress and the White House rather than relying on the good offices of the President's Science Advisor. The defense and space expenditures of the other technology-intensive countries (except the U.S.S.R.) were much lower relative to their total R&D expenditures than those of the United States, but traditional sector activities were well entrenched there also, and their science ministers found their political influence correspondingly curtailed.

---

*President Eisenhower created the post of science advisor in 1957 in response to the public shock and shift in priorities triggered by the U.S.S.R.'s Sputnik satellite. The post was abolished by President Nixon in 1973 and re-created by act of Congress in 1976 (see Chapter 9).

The year 1968 brought an abrupt leveling off of federal R&D support in the United States, and a similar decline in growth followed in other countries. While the basic cause was economic (the recession and climbing government budget deficits that started in that year), the new approach to R&D funding was rationalized by the complaint that the R&D so generously supported in the past lacked relevance to national needs and goals. While science administrators in governments and in laboratories took corrective actions designed to meet the new demand for relevance, political acceptance was slow to come, and only very recently has U.S. federal R&D support begun to rise more rapidly than it has been eroded, in real terms, by inflation.

The adjustment process took a traumatic toll. Whole laboratories were shut down or pruned beyond recognition. Research scientists and engineers were forced to find new employment outside the R&D enterprise, many of them never to return, and university enrollments in scientific and technical curricula declined drastically. Science ministers were dropped from cabinet or subcabinet status or disappeared altogether from the political scene in many countries. But "relevance" gained status as a badge of legitimacy, and the new trend in R&D program priorities regained some of the credibility with the body politic their predecessors had so comfortably enjoyed.

The Demand for Relevance

The change from "policy for science" to "science in support of public policy" has not been very effective. Certainly useful research has been done, and the reorientation of priorities that has brought unprecedented growth in government support for R&D relating to the environment, transportation, energy, and other broad social needs has been a positive development, if long overdue. However, the science policy mechanisms created by the science ministers have been least successful in dealing with the relationship of R&D to broad economic and social objectives and in devising strategies for encouraging the application of private sector technologies to these objectives. Their limited success has been further eroded by often poor implementation of the new programs by the technical agencies of government given responsibility for them.

The reasons for the apparent failure to meet the new challenge so far are several. Science and technology policy makers have generally been preoccupied with the input (funding) requirements of the R&D enterprise rather than with the delivery systems that transform the research results into technologies and products serving real needs. Science policy advisory mechanisms have continued to regard themselves as instruments for overviewing—even advocating—research programs rather than providing important analytical and factual inputs to those policy makers charged with responsibility for broad economic and social problems in which technology is a critical factor. Politicians and government officials whose expertise and preoccupations lie outside the area of technology, on the other hand, have been equally ineffectual in identifying problem-solving roles that both fully exploit the R&D community's special resources and could contribute in important ways to broader national goals. The experience of the "energy crisis" has, so far at least, diminished the stature of the science policy structure in the eyes of both politicians and the general public. R&D directed to developing new energy sources necessarily requires lead times long in terms of crisis needs. At the same time, both government officials and the R&D community lacked the analyses of the complex workings of the global energy system that might have contributed importantly to viable policy and program responses to the crisis situation.

TECHNOLOGY POLICY

Many people believe that the proper solution to these difficulties is the development of a national technology policy. What is customarily conceived here is federal action regarding technology in sectors beyond those where the federal government has a generally recognized responsibility for programing of research and development. Excluded are sectors such as defense, space, important aspects of atomic energy, and much health-related research, where the comprehensive responsibilities of the federal government are taken for granted. Included within the concept of national technology policy is the bulk of the private sector industrial activity and many public service activities, like education and transportation, where no central federal programing function has been concerned either with the activity as a whole or with its R&D components.[5]

The concept of a comprehensive national technology policy serving a broad spectrum of public needs has questionable validity. The basis for belief in the concept lies both in the recognition of the importance of technology to national goals and in the apparent successes of federal policy intervention in such sectors as defense, space, and atomic energy. This reasoning may be unsound. Technology is without question important to the achievement of national goals, but the effectiveness of a comprehensive government policy in stimulating the broader application of technology is greatly encumbered by the importance of other determining elements—the workings of the marketplace and of private capital, for instance—traditionally isolated from most forms of government intervention.

Governments are the sole market for defense technology and for much space technology. Atomic energy technology serves a special, highly aggregated market of utilities that is traditionally tightly regulated by government. Furthermore, the beginning point of atomic energy technology (and virtually its sole underpinnings during the early stages of the commercial introduction of atomic power) was wartime technology developed largely within government laboratories and long maintained in tight secrecy for national security reasons. (Even now key elements of atomic energy technology remain in government hands, e.g., fuel enrichment and radioactive waste disposal.) In the circumstances prevailing in these limited sectors, the scope for federal policy action and the assurance that policy action will be effective are clearly much greater than in areas of technological activity where the markets are disaggregated and both producers and consumers are entities outside the detailed purview of any federal government organization. Furthermore, in these broader sectors the bulk of the R&D is neither financed by nor under the overview of any federal agency.

A comprehensive national technology policy would interact with many areas of economic policy—industrial policy, fiscal and monetary policy, labor policy, policies for the regulation of public utilities, and so on—as well as with security policy, foreign policy, and many aspects of social policy. Supposing that a national technology policy were deemed feasible and useful, who would formulate it? Interpret it? Monitor its impacts? In all likelihood a comprehensive national technology policy is beyond reach. The applications of technology are too broad, involve too many decision makers in too many ways, and interact in too subtle a fashion with public interests and behavior to lend themselves to comprehensive government policy direction in a democracy.

The motivations for governments to do something to direct the energies of the civilian technology enterprise toward politically desirable goals are very strong. Lacking comprehensive policy formulations, governments have turned to less ambitious policy approaches in an attempt to influence the broad technology enterprise in specific ways. It is beyond the scope of this book to examine these various approaches in great detail, but it is valuable to identify here the principal mechanisms that have been employed. A variety of fiscal measures have been adopted to stimulate civilian technological activity in general. These include special tax treatment of private R&D and new-product introduction expenditures, grants and loans on special terms, authorization to use government-owned facilities for production for civilian markets, and tariff barriers and controls on in-bound foreign investment as a protection for infant industries. The success of these measures in stimulating private sector investment in civilian technology is difficult to judge. There is some reason to suspect that these measures provide concessional support for technological activities that might be supported from private funds in the absence of government intervention.

Government Institutions for Exploitation of Patents

Many governments (including Belgium, Canada, Denmark, Germany, Ireland, Italy, New Zealand, South Africa, Sweden, and the United Kingdom) have organized special institutions to encourage private sector exploitation of government-held patents. These agencies undertake to file and maintain patent coverage, at home and abroad, on inventions made in government-financed laboratories and to grant licenses for their use on commercial terms. If the invention clearly requires major further investment before it is ready to market, these agencies may also make low-interest loans for this purpose, to be repaid from eventual profits. The best known example is the U.K. National Research Development Corporation (NRDC), a government corporation organized in 1949 for this express purpose. (Its authority was subsequently expanded to include participation in financing applied research and development in broad areas of technology deemed important to U.K. economic objectives.) Some of the statistics relating to the NRDC are worth reviewing to gain a measure of the possibilities and the limitations of the approach.[6]

Cumulatively, from June 1949 through March 1972, NRDC was offered 12,394 patents held by U.K. government bodies, and it accepted 5,670 for commercial exploitation. (Some proportion of the latter total are privately held patents, which the NRDC also handles on a consignment basis. NRDC screened 15,522 privately held patents in addition to the government-held submissions.) On the basis of the 5,670 patents accepted for exploitation, 1,413 domestic licenses and 84 foreign licenses were successfully negotiated, of which 704 produced income.* The cumulative 23-year income from licensing is substantial—nearly £18 million. Against this one must weigh the expenses. The corresponding direct expense for patent filings and maintenance was approximately £2 million. The owners of the privately held patents involved received approximately £3 million. The administrative expense (which also covered administration of the R&D subsidy activity) amounted to roughly £10 million. A final fact is particularly interesting: A single patent (for an antibiotic) has accounted for more than half of the total cumulative licensing revenues to NRDC and only 9 patents (5 in medicine and related fields) account for 90 percent of the total revenues. While NRDC must be judged a limited success on accounting measures, its dependence on just 9 patents is a valid and typical indicator of the high risks involved if government-financed R&D is to be regarded as a profit-making investment.

Government Investment in Technology

Governments sometimes undertake to provide the financing necessary to develop new technological products believed to offer major opportunities for export income as well as a valuable stimulus to the domestic economy. Examples include the Concorde supersonic transport (a joint United Kingdom and France project); the European Airbus (France, Germany, Netherlands, and the United Kingdom); and the development of the gas centrifuge technique for uranium enrichment (Germany, Netherlands and the United Kingdom). The early support of the development of atomic power reactors by the U.S. Atomic Energy Commission is another example. The success of this approach is difficult to assess. To date, the principal customers for the technological products developed have generally been the sponsoring governments themselves, or public corporations controlled by these governments. The costs of the products to the operators (including capital costs) have frequently been so large as to require further government subsidies, at least at the early stages. Atomic power reactors might represent a success of this approach, but as I noted earlier, these might have been developed more economically and more quickly by privately financed industrial efforts if the necessary basic technology had not been sequestered for military security reasons.

---

*Foreign licensees receive the same terms as domestic licensees in NRDC practice.

In addition to the various policy instruments for government stimulation of civilian technology mentioned above, a variety of measures have been employed with the specific objective of stimulating exports. These can be regarded also as elements of a national technology policy. They are discussed briefly in Chapter 4.

INTERGOVERNMENTAL COOPERATION IN TECHNOLOGY

Before I conclude this overview of public policy bearing on the international implications of technology, it is useful to review briefly the area of bilateral and multilateral intergovernmental cooperation.

Formal intergovernmental cooperation in technological areas can serve a variety of mutual interests, complementing as well as supplementing national activities in similar fields. Its principal virtues lie in the fact that, when it is effective, intergovernmental cooperation can accomplish these things:

- Accelerate the availability of important new technologies and make their implementation possible earlier than would national efforts alone.
- Lead to earlier and greater public acceptance of new technologies.
- Focus R&D efforts in directions regarded as most promising.
- Broaden the international basis of technological know-how and experience.
- Enhance overall scientific and technological competence and encourage cooperation in other important related areas.
- Increase efficient utilization of scientists and engineers.

These attractions have led governments to expend great effort on the creation of various mechanisms for intergovernmental technological cooperation.

A bewildering array of multilateral international organizations, regional and global, deal with various policy aspects of technology.[7] The technological interests of these organizations take different forms, and it is useful to identify some of the principal international organizations involved in each of these.

1. The promotion of technology in support of particular mutual interests. This rather large and important group includes, for example:

   - The Food and Agriculture Organization of the UN, formed in 1945, among other functions promotes research in all aspects of agriculture and nutrition.

   - The International Atomic Energy Agency (IAEA) of the UN, created in 1954, is concerned with R&D in the peaceful applications of atomic energy. IAEA also administers civil nuclear safeguards, including those created by the nuclear nonproliferation treaty (see Chapter 7).

   - International Council of Scientific Unions, a nongovernmental organization that had its beginnings in 1918, has as its purpose to advance scientific progress and to coordinate inter-disciplinary and worldwide scientific projects.

   - The International Hydrographic Organization, whose antecedents date to 1889, encourages coordination of hydrographic work to advance the ease and safety of marine navigation.

2. Development and application of standards for the international utilization of technology:

   - International Telecommunications Union, dating from antecedents in 1865, undertakes the international allocation of radio frequencies.

   - International Civil Aviation Organization, formed in 1944, is concerned with the planning and development of internationally accepted methods of civil air navigation and traffic control.

   - International Bureau for the Protection of Industrial Property, organized in 1880, is concerned with international agreements regarding patents and copyrights.

   - International Bureau of Weights and Measures, formed in 1876, has as its purpose to insure international standardization of all units of measurement.

3. The application of technology to common problems:

   - World Health Organization, a specialized agency of the UN formed in 1948, conducts a variety of laboratory and field programs in the health area.

   - World Meteorological Organization (UN), with origins going back to 1878, operates a variety of facilities for weather data collection and dissemination.

- A number of organizations concerned primarily, if not exclusively, with the applications of technology to development. These are discussed in Chapter 6.

4. Consultation on rationalization of national science and technology (S&T) policies:

  - UN Educational, Scientific and Cultural Organization (UNESCO), created in 1946. Among its multiple activities it is concerned with the development of national science policies, and it has generated numerous publications in this area.

  - Organisation for Economic Co-operation and Development (OECD), formed in 1961, brings the major trading nations together for consultation on a wide variety of economic policy questions. Its principal subdivisions include the Committee on Scientific and Technological Policy, the Environment Committee, the Industry Committee, the Energy Committee, and the Nuclear Energy Agency.

These international organizations and many others not mentioned have contributed in useful ways to advancing common technological goals. Nonetheless, the results have, in every case, fallen short of what seemed possible and what was hoped for. The reasons for this shortfall are manifold; some are discussed in Chapter 9.

The general unwieldiness of multinational organizations has led many governments to turn to bilateral cooperation as a preferable alternative. Some international common interests—product standardization, for example—cannot be accomplished effectively on a bilateral basis. However, many mutual interests can be served through bilateral cooperation, and a vast network of such cooperative arrangements has come into being for this purpose. In 1976 the United States had formal bilateral agreements for science and technology cooperation with at least twenty nations,* and was engaged in eleven such agreements with the Soviet Union alone. (These data apply only to formal agreements on a government-to-government level as distinguished from agency-to-counterpart agency agreements, too numerous to keep track of.) Typically, these agreements provide for exchanges of research results, exchange visits of scientists for periods of a few weeks to a year, joint seminars and workshops, and, less frequently, specific collaborative research

---

*Argentina, Australia, Brazil, Bulgaria, Czechoslovakia, France, West Germany, Hungary, India, Italy, Japan, Korea, Mexico, New Zealand, the Philippines, Poland, Romania, Taiwan, the U.S.S.R., and Yugoslavia. An informal government-facilitated agreement is in place with the People's Republic of China.

projects. Costs of participation are borne by the funding agencies of the two governments, each paying the costs incurred by its own participants.

Frequently the primary motivation behind such agreements is political. An agreement to cooperate in S&T matters is widely understood to signal the existence (or intention) of friendly relations between the two nations and thus serves domestic and international political purposes. Often agreements of this type have very little substantive effect, simply serving to legitimize politically the informal S&T cooperation already existing between counterpart research organizations, universities, and individual scientists, and technological relationships in the industrial sector. Some bilateral cooperative programs are of considerable substantive importance, however, contributing importantly to technological progress on both sides. It should be recognized that the realization of political benefits rests on the achievement of substantive results of interest to both sides, but involves much more.

While formal bilateral and multilateral R&D cooperation seems to be firmly established as a vehicle of international political relations, it is difficult to describe convincingly the nature of the process that links cooperative S&T activity to explicit political goals. Foreign policy has as its goals the accomplishment of certain international outcomes that may consist of setting in train particular political or social processes, redistribution of physical or economic goods, formal agreement to mutually undertake specific responsibilities or to forego specific unilateral actions, and so on. How can the joint pursuit of S&T influence these goals, and what strategies for the planning and conduct of cooperative activities offer the greatest promise for achieving the desired political outcomes? This question can be addressed by considering the following chain of relationships, where the arrows indicate the direction of influence:[8]

research strategy ———> research results ———>
policy consequences ———> international outcomes

International outcomes are the product of many influences, but the ones most susceptible to the impact of cooperative S&T activity are those structured by formal intra- and intergovernmental policy formulations by public officials operating within a preexisting political and institutional framework. Linkage between cooperative and specific international outcomes can only derive from the consequences of the activity perceived by policy makers and impacting on institutional behavior. The S&T strategy, then, should be chosen so that the results of cooperative S&T will lead to policy impacts favorable to achievement of the desired international outcome.

It may be objected that basic research (in the hard sciences, at least) doesn't lead to such results, but that view rests on too narrow a conception of research results. The results of research are not simply new data or hypotheses; the broader experience, enlarged perspectives, and new personal and institutional relationships are equally important results of research. The implications of the whole array of research results—substantive and subjective, direct and indirect—for the premises on which policies are founded, on the constraints and opportunities for policy formulation, and on the perspectives of policy makers are the operative factors here. By extension, S&T strategy in this context implies far more than the formulation of hypotheses and research protocols; it must concern itself with the sociology of the R&D environment as well.

These things are easy to say and easy to agree with, but very hard to do much about. Nonetheless, if the pursuit of cooperative S&T in the furtherance of foreign policy goals is to continue and to prove worthwhile, those responsible for its stimulation, planning, monitoring, and evaluation must seek to understand the nature of the chain of relationships sketched above and to develop the concepts and techniques that give it operative validity.

Generally, the most substantive bilateral technology programs link counterpart technical agencies in the two countries. In the United States NASA and the Department of Energy are each actively engaged in dozens of such arrangements, many of them central to the accomplishment of their mission objectives. The Department of Interior is steadily increasing the number and scope of its bilateral programs, particularly in the areas of geology and water resource management.

Even the best bilateral technological programs suffer from a major constraint. To date, it has proven very difficult, if not impossible, to work out satisfactory arrangements for engaging the private sector—an essential step when the technology involved has significant industrial and commercial applications. This problem should be capable of solution, but the sad fact is that, in the United States, at least, it hasn't yet been addressed in a competent and forthright fashion.

The following chapters take up specific aspects of the interaction between technology and international relations. Conflicting national interests, especially those that involve government and industry, are a common theme. Public policy issues of great complexity crop up everywhere. Bilateral and multilateral international intergovernmental institutional arrangements have evolved, but in each case with limited success.

Notes

1. *The Gaps in Technology Between Member Countries.* A series of eight reports. Paris: Organisation for Economic Co-operation and Development, 1968.
2. Servan-Schreiber, Jean-Jacques. *The American Challenge.* New York: Atheneum, 1968. For a different perspective see Rene Foch, *Europe and Technology.* Paris: Atlantic Institute, 1970.
3. Estimates by the Stockholm Institute for Strategic Studies, 1970.
4. Unless otherwise indicated, all funding data in this chapter are from *Annual Surveys of Science Resources.* Washington, D.C.: National Science Foundation.
5. This definition is adapted from Richard R. Nelson, Organizational Requirements for a National Technology Policy (unpublished), February 1974. The paragraphs that follow draw heavily on Professor Nelson's insights; the biases are my own.
6. Data are from the *Annual Report* of the National Research Development Corporation for 1973.
7. A useful listing of those IOs to which the U.S. government contributes funds directly can be found in the *Annual Report on U.S. Contributions to International Organizations . . .* [published] *pursuant to Section 2 of Public Law 806, 81st Congress.* This publication appears as a House Document of the Committee on International Relations.
8. This formulation follows David B. Bobrow, *Technology-Related International Outcomes: R&D Strategies to Induce Sound Public Policy.* Pittsburgh, Pa.: International Studies Association, 1974.

4

TECHNOLOGY, TRADE, AND MULTINATIONAL ENTERPRISE

The role of technology in the global development of trade, investment, and multinational enterprise since World War II is profound. The fact that more than three decades have gone by since the last "world war"—a longer interval than any other in the last two centuries—is perhaps in large part the result of the growth-inducing impact of rapidly increasing international trade and foreign investment and the new perceptions of global interdependence that have accompanied this growth. The dramatic emergence of multinational corporations and the domination of world trade and investment patterns these institutions have achieved is both a source and a result of international interdependence. This chapter explores the factors involved and their implications for public policy.

TRADE

Since World War II world trade has expanded rapidly, increasing fivefold from 1950 to 1974. (Instabilities provoked by the oil price rise and the world recession set in in 1974; the near-term future remains uncertain.) U.S. exports have accounted for 12–15 percent of the total world exports throughout the last decade, in *absolute* terms a far larger share than that of any other single country, and about two-

48

thirds of the share of the European Community as a group (excluding intracommunity trade).[1] At the same time, because U.S. gross national product (GNP) is so much larger than that of any other nation—24 percent of world GNP and larger than that of the combined European Community (1975)—the proportion of U.S. production of goods that goes to exports is smaller than that of other trading nations. The 1975 percentages of production for export were: United States, 10 percent; European Community (net of intratrade), 11 percent; Japan, 22 percent; and Canada, 32 percent.* The absorptive capacity of our domestic economy is so large and our industrial and agricultural production are so strong and so diversified that we have not yet felt the pressures to export for the purposes of sustaining economic growth that bear heavily on other nations.

Other major trading nations have also been forced to concentrate on exports in order to pay for the large imports of food, fuels, and raw materials they require. Until fairly recently the United States felt comparatively little pressure from this direction. Our export earnings were large enough to cover imports of essential materials for which domestic supplies were inadequate plus a far larger amount for discretionary imports of consumer items (from exotic foodstuffs to cameras and sport cars), and still leave a comfortable trade surplus to cover such overseas expenditures as foreign aid, military assistance, and tourism.

This happy situation can no longer be relied on. In 1971, for the first time since 1893, U.S. foreign trade was in deficit—imports exceeded exports by $2 billion. The unprecedented corrective measures taken in mid-1971—wage and price controls, a temporary import surcharge, and, most important, the devaluation of the dollar—brought a reversal of the trend, yielding a trade surplus of more than $11 billion for 1975. The underlying trends (other than exchange rates, which had become increasingly artificial since the late 1960s but may be heading toward equilibrium now) still remain, and the U.S. trade deficit exceeded $30 billion in 1977. (The largest contribution to this result came from petroleum imports, which, by 1977, had reached $45 billion; they were a little over $8 billion in 1973, before the OPEC embargo.)

The two major factors in the deterioration of the U.S. foreign trade position are the escalating import cost of fuels and raw materials and the decreasing competitiveness of non-technology-intensive U.S.–manufactured goods in both domestic and foreign

---

*Ratios of this type can be calculated with equal validity in several different ways; thus the figures given here may not agree with figures published elsewhere. They are properly indicative of the underlying point, however.

Table 4.1
Average Annual Rate of Increase in Manufacturing Productivity*

	1960–1965	1965–1970	1970–1975
United States	4.5%	1.3%	1.4%
France	5.2	6.5	2.4
Germany	6.4	5.2	4.5
Italy	7.1	5.2	4.4
Japan	8.5	13.1	4.1
United Kingdom	3.8	3.4	2.6

*Real output per man-hour.
  Source: *International Economic Report of the President,* 1976, p. 78

markets. Although the U.S. has earned a substantial (and generally increasing) income from the export of minerals, fuels, and other raw materials since Colonial times, U.S. imports in these categories have exceeded exports for several decades. The deficit increased rather steadily until 1970. Since then, and particularly since the quantum jump in the price of imported petroleum in 1973, the deficit has increased rapidly, to $33.5 billion in 1976.

Because of the decreasing competitiveness of U.S. non-technology-intensive manufactured goods, the trade deficit in that category has developed more rapidly than in the raw materials area. We enjoyed a trade surplus in low-technology goods until 1959; in 1975 the trade deficit in this category was nearly $6.3 billion.* There are several reasons for this development, including artificial exchange rates that made foreign goods cheaper relative to U.S. products in both U.S. and foreign markets and the rapidly improving quality and attractiveness of many consumer products manufactured overseas. (As individual customers U.S. citizens unquestionably benefited from the availability of cheap, good-quality imports, but there was an adverse impact on those sectors of the U.S. economy whose goods these imports displaced.) The most disturbing reason for this trend, however, and in the longer term the most important, is the decline in the productivity of U.S. manufacturing labor relative to labor in other manufacturing countries. Since 1950 the United States has consistently invested a far smaller proportion of GNP in new productive capacity than any of the other major exporters ex-

---

*This category includes: steel products; textiles, clothing, and footwear; and consumer electronics. Nearly half of the deficit is in the second group.

cept the United Kingdom. The impact on manufacturing output per man-hour is evident in Table 4.1. In general, manufacturing wage rates have also risen much faster in these other countries than in the United States, however.

TECHNOLOGY AND THE U.S. BALANCE OF TRADE

In contrast to U.S. trade deficits in raw materials and non-technology-intensive manufactured goods are the surpluses generated by the export of the products of U.S. advanced technology. Figures 4.1 and 4.2 compare the historic trade performance of selected commodities in technology-intensive categories with examples in non-technology-intensive categories. The developing trends are clearly evident. A rising surplus trend is clear in Figure 4.1 for nonelectrical machinery (a category that includes machine tools, chemical plants, and nuclear reactors). Figure 4.2 reveals sharply developing downward trends in motor vehicles, steel products,* consumer electronics, and apparel items. The detailed future behavior of both sets of curves may be affected by changes in currency exchange rates, but no foreseeable development in exchange rates could alter the basic tendencies evident here. Only a relative decline in U.S. technological leadership, which is possible, would change this situation.

Any discussion of the role of advanced technology in U.S. world trade would be incomplete without a mention of agricultural products. In 1960 U.S. agriculture imports and exports were in balance. In subsequent years both imports and exports have risen, but exports have grown much more rapidly than imports. The resulting trade surplus reached $12.4 billion in 1975.† Despite import quotas and other trade barriers erected by the European Community to protect its own farmers, a significant portion of total U.S. agricultural output goes to exports: 17 percent of fruit production, 33 percent of cotton and corn, 42 percent of tobacco, and more than 60 percent of

---

*The rise in the curve for steel products in 1973 proved to be transitory. The steel industry has suffered a worldwide decline since 1974, and the United States has suffered more than most.

†The sharp rise in 1972 and beyond reflects heavy wheat purchases by the U.S.S.R. The long-term future of this trade cannot be certain, but Soviet per capita consumption is rising as a result of more grain-fed meat in the diet, and the Soviet wheat-growing regions are more susceptible to bad growing weather than are those of the United States (see James E. Newman and Robert C. Pickett, World Climates and Food Supply Variations, *Science*, 1974, **186,** 877).

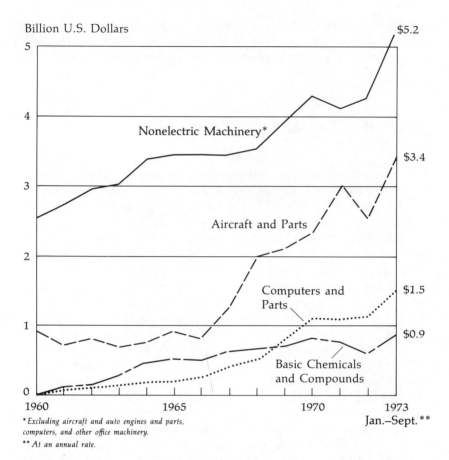

Billion U.S. Dollars

Figure 4.1
U.S. Trade Balance in Selected High-Technology Commodities (Source: *International Economic Report of the President*, 1974, p. 38).

wheat and soybeans. The United States is, of course, blessed with an abundance of fertile land and an unusually good growing climate, in world terms. These natural advantages have been greatly enhanced by the amazing rise in productivity of U.S. farm workers. In constant dollars the value of production per worker grew from $2700 in 1950 to $6600 in 1970. This increase in productivity came from improvements in farm machinery and especially from technological improvements in seeds, fertilizers, insecticides, and irrigation techniques. These improvements require capital. Capital investment per U.S. farm worker reached an estimated $6000 in the early 1970s, as compared with $200 per worker in Japan. (This comparison is not the only meaningful one, however. On a capital in-

Billion U.S. Dollars

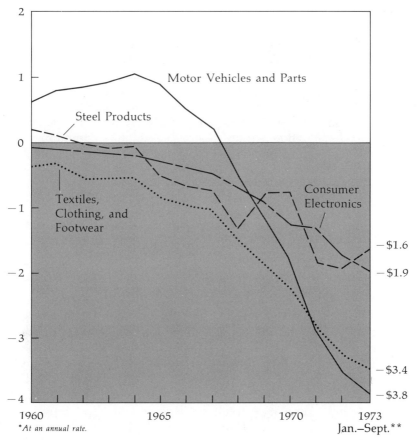

Figure 4.2
U.S. Trade Balance in Selected Low-Technology Commodities (Source: *International Economic Report of the President*, 1974, p. 38).

vestment *per acre* basis, Japan led the United States $300 to $110. Because Japanese farming is more intensive, the dollar value of its agricultural output per acre exceeds that of the United States.)

The clear implication of all these statistics is that the future of U.S. exports depends on continued U.S. leadership in advanced technology, providing, of course, that the United States continues to enjoy relatively free access to foreign markets for its products.[2]

That our export trade is vital to our broader economic future is evident in the rising costs of our imports of critical raw materials, including fuels. Since the Kennedy Round of multilateral tariff negotiations in the 1960s, the global economy has been moving generally in the direction of freer trade. There is room for further movement, however, and this would be to the advantage of the United States as well as other countries. The average tariffs for imports subject to duty of the industrialized countries (in 1971) were 5.7 percent for raw materials, 10.5 percent for semifinished manufactured products, and 11.3 percent for finished manufactured products.[3] Tariffs are not the only measure of freedom of trade; import and export quotas, national preferences in government purchasing, and other nontariff barriers become increasingly important as duties are reduced. A national trade policy based on a commitment to maximum freedom of trade must recognize that as the socialist bloc and the less developed countries come increasingly into the world trading system, the ideal of a free-trade market may be less and less politically sustainable, at home and abroad.

FOREIGN INVESTMENT

Along with international trade, direct foreign investment is of rapidly increasing importance to the U.S. economy, and is highly dependent on U.S. technological leadership. Cumulative U.S. direct investment abroad rose from $32 billion in 1960 to $133 billion in 1975. The corresponding direct investment income rose from $2.4 billion to $18.2 billion in the same interval.* At year end 1975, U.S. direct investments in manufacturing capabilities accounted for 45 percent of the cumulative total, while petroleum and mining investments accounted for 31 percent and 13 percent, respectively. Manufacturing has accounted for an increasing share of U.S. foreign investment in recent years, as opportunities for increased investment in petroleum and mining have diminished and as a result of the growing importance of the technology that generally accompanies direct investments in manufacturing. The shift toward emphasis on manufacturing is accompanied by increased emphasis on the industrialized countries as the locale for new investment. In the

---

*In the usage of economists, *direct* foreign investment refers to investments in specific enterprises that are accompanied by management control of the enterprise by the investor. *Portfolio* investments, in contrast, are investments in stocks and bonds issued by such enterprises that represent so small a proportion of the total shares, or *debt paper,* issued that the investor does not obtain any direct management control of the enterprise as a corollary of investment. For statistical reporting purposes, most governments define investment representing less than 10 percent of the outstanding shares of a particular enterprise as a portfolio investment.

1960–1972 interval 73 percent of new investment went to the developed countries. (Canada's share of new U.S. investment in this period was about one-third, representing a slight decline as compared with earlier years, when U.S. firms had invested heavily in Canadian mining enterprises.)

Direct investment in foreign manufacturing and distribution enterprises generally reflects a strategy of horizontal integration—the pursuit of broader markets for existing products and services—as against vertical integration—extending the productive scope of the enterprise to incorporate processing steps previously provided by subcontractors. Horizontal integration is the principal strategy pursued by multinational enterprises.

INTERNATIONAL MOVEMENT OF TECHNOLOGY

So far we have focused on trade in tangible goods—foodstuffs, raw and processed fuels and materials, and the products of technology. There is another category of "goods" in international trade that has assumed dramatically increasing importance since World War II, to the point where it has become a major preoccupation of governments: trade in patents, trademarks, and proprietary design and production know-how. International transfer of technology through commercial and industrial channels is a dominant feature of international relations, giving rise to important political, economic, and security issues.

Industrial technology is transferred internationally in a wide variety of ways. The most pervasive, and the least contentious in international political terms, is the diffusion from producers to users that is implicit in the sale and use of products and services that embody the technology. Cumulatively, the amount of technology transferred in this manner is very large and has enormous influence on patterns of industrial and commercial development worldwide. A few examples will serve to illustrate the point.

The developers and producers of synthetic yarns, largely concentrated in the United States and a few Western European countries, have introduced these products to textile industries throughout the world with great success. They have, of necessity, taught their customers all that the producers know (from their own R&D, but equally importantly from their contact with their other customers in the textile industry) about the possibilities for exploiting the unique properties of these synthetics in textile products. This represents a massive international transfer of technology, but one so complex in character as to defy specific description or analysis and thus beyond the reach of government controls should governments see reasons for attempting to invoke them. An analagous mass diffusion of modern technology has occurred as a result of international trade in electronic components, particularly semiconductor devices, including transistors and integrated circuits. Still another example is the transfer of technology that accompanies trade in machine tools and production machinery of all types.

More conspicuous to policy makers is the transfer of technology through the licensing by technology-originating firms to unaffiliated foreign firms of patents, product designs, process methods, and other forms of proprietary know-how. This form of international trade goes back at least a century, but it has surged forward since World War II, in response to the development of national industrial and investment strategies established originally by Japan, most conspicuously, and adopted by a number of other nations who sought the most rapid available means to overcome the technology gaps resulting from the destructive impacts of the war or, in the less developed countries, from earlier colonial economic policies.

The most important mechanism for the international transfer of industrial technology in recent decades has been the operations of multinational corporations—MNCs or MNEs (for enterprises) as they are commonly called in Europe. I will have more to say in succeeding sections about this phenomenon and the international political issues its dramatic evolution has led to. My immediate purpose is to examine some of the broader international political implications of the international transfer of technology on this historically unprecedented scale. I will concentrate on the transfer of technology to foreign producing enterprises, setting aside for the moment the transfer of technology to consumers that, as pointed out earlier, is an implicit corollary of international trade in tangible goods.

International trade in technology per se raises a number of political questions in both the domestic and international contexts. Domestically, the political debate about exports of technology centers on five concerns:

- The possibility that the international transfer of technology by domestic firms (through licensing or direct foreign investment) amounts to "exporting jobs."

- The possibility that this process will accelerate the development of foreign competition in the world market for U.S. exports.
- The possibility that U.S. technology-exporting firms are setting too low a price on the technology involved by basing their decisions on individual corporate interests rather than on national interests.
- The possibility that the export of U.S. technology will ultimately result in an "international division of labor," which would narrow the base of the national economy with resulting serious implications for economic and military security.
- The possibility that the technology exported by U.S. firms for ostensible application to civilian products will, in fact, be turned to military purposes by potential adversaries.

Export of Jobs

The leaders of organized labor and some of their supporters in the Congress and elsewhere have argued strongly that a major effect of the export of U.S. technology is a reduction in job opportunities for U.S. workers. This happens, they claim, in the licensing of unaffiliated foreign firms, the creation of foreign manufacturing subsidiaries by U.S. firms, the joint production of high-technology products by U.S. and foreign firms, or the increasing practice of sending semifinished components and subassemblies outside the country for the labor-intensive phases of assembly, followed by reimport into the United States—a practice widely followed in the semiconductor industry. The validity of this proposition defies objective analysis and proof or disproof since so many factors extraneous to the particular issue can have equal and perhaps greater influence on U.S. exports or domestic employment. This proposition, like so many others in the socioeconomic area, must remain inextricably in the "what if?" category. However, there is ample and incontestable statistical evidence that the exports of U.S. corporations with manufacturing subsidiaries in foreign countries, to those same countries, have consistently grown at a faster rate than the exports of nonmultinational U.S. firms operating in the same technological sectors and markets.[4]

This result should not be unexpected; by establishing manufacturing, distribution, and service capabilities in a particular national market, the MNC becomes, from the customers' standpoint, a domestic supplier to that market and thus to be preferred to a supplier relying solely on import sources. The resulting customer preference understandably extends to some degree to the MNC's entire product line, including those items it imports from its home country as well as those manufactured indigenously. This kind of argument can hardly be expected to settle to everyone's satisfaction the "export of jobs" issue. It is appropriate to ask, however, whether the exported jobs—if they exist—are jobs that U.S. factory workers would wish to fill at wage rates that would make the products competitive in the world market.

Strengthening Foreign Competition

It is impossible to argue that the international diffusion of technology does not strengthen the productive enterprises of the technology-receiving countries. This is not to say, however, that on balance the international export of U.S. technology weakens the competitive position of the U.S. industrial economy in the world market. In fact, there are persuasive arguments to the contrary. To the extent that the recipient economy is strengthened, its purchasing power is strengthened, so that the total world market is increased. To the extent that it is U.S. technology that is adopted by foreign producers, the markets supplied by those producers are further "Americanized," that is, they become more committed to U.S. standards of design, production, and use and thus increasingly receptive to products of U.S. origin.

Furthermore, there is considerable logic behind, and objective evidence in support of, the product-cycle theory, which argues that it is not the latest technology that is exported but rather the older technology, which is exported in response to the pressure of newer technology to displace it in the domestic market.[5] So long as the United States maintains its past dynamism in the development and market exploitation of technological innovation, there seem to be few objective grounds for arguing that the export of U.S. technology is (in the absence of other factors that may distort the situation) leading to a decline in the U.S. competitive position in world markets. It may be noted that the revenues earned by U.S. firms from the exploitation of their technology abroad are themselves an important reason that R&D investment by U.S. firms in relationship to gross sales revenues continues to exceed that of any other country.

Pricing of Technology Exports

There are many influential people, in and out of government, who believe that U.S. industrial firms export their technology too cheaply, responding to immediate business considerations and a "marginal pricing" psychology that may be contrary to the U.S. national interest. The evidence available to support this thesis is at best sketchy and anecdotal. The rapid economic growth of Japan, drawing heavily on technology obtained by licensing agreements with U.S. firms, is often cited as a case in point. This argument, as in the case of so many others offered in support of this proposition, overlooks the profound influence of a variety of other factors in the Japanese case: the extraordinary rate of fixed capital formation, the unique experience of the Japanese in producing for export markets, the extremely low economic base from which the war-torn Japanese economy commenced its fantastic growth performance, etc. The Japanese example also ignores the fact that during the late 1940s and the 1950s, successive U.S. administrations declared it to be in the U.S. national interest to provide Japan with industrial technology on financial terms that sometimes approached the concessional category.

Nonetheless, the feeling remains strong among some officials that the U.S. government should intervene in the export of industrial technology so as to insure a fair market price. This argument is applied particularly to those areas of technology to which the U.S. government has provided a particular economic stimulus through R&D and production contracts. "R&D recoupment" is the specific justification generally applied to proposals of this kind.*

In fact, the larger procurement contracts of the federal technical agencies generally provide for pro-rata recovery of nonrecurring costs, including R&D investment, originally funded by the government when the particular product involved is also sold to nongovernment customers, including foreign buyers. The allocation, which may cover initial production tooling and set-up costs as well as R&D, is generally small. The application of this procedure to the export (or other sale) of technology per se encounters substantial practical difficulties:[6]

---

*R&D recoupment, in this context, refers to the recovery by the government from the contractor of a lump sum or pro-rata amount representing repayment of a portion of the government's R&D investment when the resulting product is sold or the design technology licensed to nongovernmental buyers.

- The very fact that the firm in question was awarded an R&D contract represents an implicit acknowledgment of the depth and breadth of its preexisting expertise in the areas of technology involved. In such circumstances how can the government's contribution to the particular technology to be sold be distinguished from the firm's independent and proprietary contribution?

- Technology can be transferred by way of patents, manufacturing drawings, and process specifications; through on-the-job training and technical assistance; through management contracts; and so on. In which of these areas is the government able to assert a definable property right? It might be argued that the government's property rights are embodied solely in patents for inventions arising from contract-supported R&D. In fact, the standard provisions of the vast majority of U.S. government R&D contracts reserve to the government only a right to royalty-free use of the patented invention in contract procurement for government use, the rights to commercial exploitation going to the industrial contractor. When the government agency does take title to the patent rights, historic U.S. policy and practice is to file the patent only in the United States. When that is the case, the patented invention can be produced outside the United States by any person or firm without violating any U.S. or foreign law.

- If the industrial firm is regarded as unwilling or unable to exact a fair market price from a foreign purchaser of the technology in question, who can? Intervention in the negotiations by government representatives does not increase the value of the technology to a foreign purchaser, it can only increase the price. As a practical matter, the likely outcome is that the U.S. supplier of the technology will have to pay the share of the sales price demanded by the government out of the return it would otherwise have gotten for itself. This may serve the taxpayers' interests, but it does not strengthen the relative competitive position of the U.S. economy or of the firm involved.

Narrowing the U.S. Technological Base

The concern has been expressed, particularly by the Department of Defense, that the export of U.S. technology may lead to U.S. industry's eventual abandonment of particular areas of technology, to the detriment of our economic and military security. The validity of this concern is as difficult to evaluate as that of some of the other concerns identified above. First of all, sellers of a technology obviously still retain their knowledge of it and usually also the right to exploit it for their own purposes. It is certainly true that some technologies in which the United States once held a strong position of leadership—radio receiving tubes, for example—are no longer actively pursued in the United States, although they still receive attention in some other countries (in this instance the Soviet Union). The example cited, standing alone, hardly provides a basis for concern; the exploitation of radio receiving tube technology was abandoned because it was displaced by an enormously superior new technology. It is possible, of course, that instances of abandonment may arise that would be significant to our national security, although it is highly improbable that any successful technology would be abandoned unless either its market was to disappear or it was displaced by a superior technology. Neither of these circumstances would suggest that abandonment adversely impacted on our national interests.

The preceding paragraphs relate to key political issues in the international transfer of technology as perceived by domestic policy makers, particularly those of the technology-supplying nation. The policy makers in technology-receiving nations have concerns too, and these should be mentioned before we move on. (Those especially relevant to the less developed countries are dealt with at some length in Chapter 6. The focus here is on the advanced countries, although some of the issues raised apply to the less developed as well). It is possible to be more brief here than in the preceding section because, in large degree, the domestic political concerns of technology-receiving countries are the obverse of those of technology-supplying countries, so the detail above is often relevant to both perspectives.

The principal policy concerns of technology-receiving countries can be grouped into three broad areas:

- Technological dependency.
- The possibility that heavy reliance on imported technology acts to suppress indigenous R&D and innovative activity.
- The risks of market dominance by foreign technology suppliers.

Technological dependence is no straw man, even for the advanced countries. Particularly when the technology is supplied through a local subsidiary of a multinational firm, the technology-importing nation may find that its reliance on a foreign source for a specific technology tends to grow and broaden, uncontrollably, to similar reliance on a wide range of the supplier's proprietary technology. The problems Western Europe has encountered because of early reliance on IBM in the computer market and on Motorola and Texas Instruments in the semiconducter market are illustrative. The fact that Japan, while relying very heavily on imported technology in the post–World War II years, seems now to be independently developing the technology needed in its priority industrial areas is probably evidence more of the unique character of Japanese government-industry relationships than of failures in Western European policy. Western Europe has taken strenuous measures to avoid or mitigate the threat of technological dependence in priority industrial sectors, with mixed success. Efforts in the computer sector, which ranged from massive subsidies to more or less forced mergers among European Community industrial firms, have only just begun to show promise of success. Joint government sponsorship of a variety of aerospace projects has cost European taxpayers a great deal of money with little reward but pride. On the other hand, U.K.-German-Dutch partnership in the development of the centrifuge technique for uranium enrichment (see Chapter 7) has been a great technological success, although the payoff is still to come.

The suppressive effect of reliance on imported technology on indigenous R&D is of special concern to the less developed countries, but it is often raised as a problem in the advanced countries as well, particularly in Europe. The argument goes that imported technology, usually chosen because it is already well established in the source market and perhaps in third-country markets as well, tends to close out opportunities for indigenous innovations, particularly those that might otherwise be offered by small entrepreneurial firms. Associated with this argument is the proposition that foreign technology suppliers tend to take advantage of their local contacts to hire away the most promising local scientists and engineers—this is the "brain drain" concern. It is difficult to evaluate the reality of either of these notions, since both are in the "what if?" category. In all likelihood, whatever validity these arguments have is a narrow consideration in the context of a very complex situation.

The concern that foreign technology-supplying firms achieve a dominant position in the local market is related to the technology dependency argument, though it calls on other arguments as well. Certainly a decision to import technology usually, though not always, means that it or a suitable alternative is not available locally. This implies that the importer expects the imported technology to achieve at least temporary market dominance. Imported technology is also firm-specific; that is, it is proprietary to a particular supplying firm and thus carries to the local market a product identity. (Frequently this is made explicit by licensing arrangements providing for the importer's use of an associated brand name.) These ingredients are indeed among those from which a dominant market position is created, but their presence by no means guarantees that market dominance will, in fact, occur. In any event, market dominance fears, like the concerns mentioned earlier, are most real when technology is imported via a subsidiary of a multinational firm. We will explore the nature and impact of such firms in greater depth below.

MULTINATIONAL CORPORATIONS

No attempt to describe the interaction of technology with international relations can ignore the multinational corporation. In the scale and breadth of their activities and in their relative freedom to pursue purely pragmatic strategies, MNCs are increasingly more important to the substance of international technological relations than are the activities of governments themselves. To cite a nontypical example, IBM enjoys 60 percent or more of the market for computers in every one of the countries in which it has manufacturing and marketing subsidiaries except the United Kingdom, where its market share is 40 percent. MNCs as a group control one-fifth or more of the European Community markets for a wide range of high-technology products.

There are various ways to define what is meant by an MNC. For the purposes of this book, with its focus on technology, an MNC can be considered a business enterprise that exerts direct control of subsidiaries, combining, as a minimum, manufacturing and marketing functions, located in one or more foreign countries. This definition would eliminate, for example, those offshore operations that engage solely in limited fabrication and assembly operations, such as the semiconductor and radio–TV assembly operations conducted by many U.S. firms in Singapore, Hong Kong, Taiwan, and Mexico; and organizations that perform a purely commercial or service function (banks, insurance companies, hotel chains, etc.).

Even with this limiting definition, MNCs exhibit considerable diversity not only in product lines and marketing and distribution arrangements but also in the nature and degree of local management control. IBM, for example, operates in a highly integrated fashion and employs sophisticated management systems, of American origin, in each subsidiary. ITT (which originated in Europe but is now U.S.–based) and Philips (Netherlands-based) operate essentially as loose assemblages—for capital utilization and profit consolidation purposes—of individual operations that otherwise behave much like their local competitors. The significance of these various corporate strategies in international technological relations is considerable.

MNCs are by no means a new phenomenon, nor is their impact on international relations a new issue. We have only to recall the Dutch East Indies Company or the Hudson's Bay Company to be certain of that. Nonetheless, with the internationalization of the market, the sources, and the factors of production of high-technology goods since World War II, the international political issues surrounding MNCs have taken on a new character and a new urgency.

MNCs and Technology

In high-technology sectors MNCs are dominant in virtually every important respect.* As a group they include the largest firms in their business areas, spend the highest amounts on R&D, have the highest exports, and enjoy the highest growth rates in both domestic and export sales. MNCs give governments problems, but they are here to stay and there is every reason to believe that they will continue the performance leadership they have shown in the last decades. If MNCs did not exist, a hundred bright young executives around the world would be busy, right now, inventing them.

A 1975 survey by the Commission of the European Communities provides some impressive data.[7] There were then approximately 10,000 MNCs, with 2,570 based in the United States and 4,534 based in the European Community. The latter have 49,256 subsidiaries abroad, while the former have 24,117. Of the European Community MNCs, 173 have subsidiaries in 20 or more countries; 113 U.S. MNCs are similarly ubiquitous. The 1,202 U.S. MNCs in manufacturing had 1973 gross sales of $670 billion; the 2,493 European MNCs in manufacturing had sales of $469 billion. Over half of the top 200 MNCs are U.S.–based. These top 200 had combined sales of nearly one-third of the combined GNPs of all OECD countries. One final eye opener: MNCs employ one-eighth of the total labor force of the OECD countries.

---

*There are exceptions. The aerospace industry is virtually devoid of MNCs, presumably because of its close ties to national defense, though international coproduction arrangements are common.

MNCs are, without question, the most important vehicle for the international diffusion of industrial technology. At least 90 percent of net revenues to U.S. firms from foreign use of their technologies goes to MNCs. MNC returns on transferred technology are very high. Though many U.S. firms make important use of foreign-generated technology, inbound royalties on technology exceed outbound royalties by 10 to 1. The net inbound royalties for exported technology were $2.3 billion in 1971 (90 percent of this in MNC intracompany transactions). This amount represented 11 percent of total U.S. industrial R&D expenditures in that year and more than one-quarter of industrially financed R&D.[8]

High technology MNCs are overwhelmingly the most important R&D spenders. In 1966 (the most recent year for which data are available) U.S. MNCs accounted for the following percentages of total industrial R&D outlays in the technology-intensive sectors:

Chemicals and drugs	86%
Instruments	85
Primary and fabricated metals	81
Rubber products	71
Nonelectrical machinery	57
Electrical machinery	51

MNC returns on overseas investment are not high by the standards the stock market, at least, would prefer to apply, averaging 9.6 percent of book value for the subsidiaries of U.S. MNCs located in the advanced countries and 11 percent for those in the developing countries (1965–1968 data). Overseas investment by U.S. MNCs is growing at a faster rate than their domestic investments, particularly among high-technology MNCs. For the 1966–1970 period, however, new direct investment overseas still averaged only about one-quarter of new direct investment in U.S. operations. (For low-technology U.S. MNCs the corresponding figure is about 10 percent.)

MNCs have shown a remarkable rate of growth in total foreign sales (exports plus subsidiary sales to non-U.S. buyers). In the last decade the annual foreign sales growth of U.S. MNCs in manufacturing has averaged 7.9 percent.[9] The growth in sales by foreign subsidiaries has not, however, resulted in decreasing MNC export sales. On the contrary, MNCs easily outdistance their non-MNC competitors in export volume (as a percentage of domestic production) and the rate of export sales growth. It is sometimes argued that U.S. exports are not as large as they might be if U.S.–based MNCs did not manufacture overseas, but the proposition, which is in the category of "what if?" problems, is not subject to verification. The U.S. Tariff Commission estimates that 18 percent of the sales of the foreign subsidiaries of U.S.–based MNCs ($14 billion in 1970) is an upper limit for the possible loss of U.S. exports arising from these foreign operations. For comparison the growth in the sales of the foreign subsidiaries of U.S. MNCs from 1960 to 1970 was $53 billion.

It is probable that, as a matter of business strategy, MNCs do not generally export their latest, first-line technology. In the first place, the introduction of a new technology is a high-risk activity, and most corporate managers will prefer to undertake it in the closest possible proximity to the R&D group that developed it and to the most experienced production team, which invariably means the parent operation. In the second place, one of the important intangibles accounting for the success of U.S.–based MNCs is the widespread (if sometimes reluctant) conviction of most foreign markets that "U.S. technology is best." Taking maximum advantage of this perception means establishing the product in the United States before introducing it to overseas manufacture.

How MNCs Transfer Technology

Technology is transferred through MNCs from the parent to the host country in a variety of ways. The use of patented technology and the production of proprietary product designs, the utilization of proprietary methods and processes, and the associated training of local staff constitute collectively the most basic and probably the most important vehicles for transfer. Basic and applied research conducted by the subsidiary operation—often cited by host government spokesmen as the vehicle most important to their interests—as such transfers no technology to the indigenous economy. Research is essentially an intracorporate activity unless and until the results are transferred to the local marketplace through the resulting products and services or as individual scientists and engineers who have participated take up employment with local competitors. As we will see later, the corporate decision to undertake research in a foreign location is usually motivated by factors other than the size of the host market for its potential results. Product and process development and adaptation, which are inherently market-oriented, are the usual R&D emphasis of the foreign subsidiaries and do result in the transfer of technology, sometimes on a massive scale.

A great deal of technology is transferred—to the local marketplace, to other local producers, or to the local infrastructure—by a variety of routes.[10] One obvious mechanism is the mobility of employees at all levels from production workers to general managers among firms engaged in similar activities. In many countries, however, the high mobility of industrial employees characteristic of the United States is inconsistent with deeply rooted social tradition and may sometimes be severely constrained by law. Other mechanisms, of greater or less significance depending on the nature of the technology involved and the special character of the host economy, include:

- Local purchasing and subcontracting. For high-technology products, the purchase from outside sources of special materials, components, tooling, piece parts, and subassemblies is necessarily subjected to tight specifications and quality assurance measures. These procedures inevitably transfer significant technology from buyer to supplier; so much so, in fact, that information derived from this source is a major source of "industrial intelligence" in many countries.

- Customer engineering. High-technology products require, for their successful use, that appropriate customer personnel be familiarized fully with the performance capabilities and appropriate applications of the product, operating and service procedures. This process, which in the case of computers, aircraft, or automatic machine tools, for instance, is very extensive, results in important transfers of technology.

- Market rationalization. Many high-technology products can be exploited by their users only when either a formal or a de facto comprehensive pattern of standards governs the complex interfaces between the product and the ancillary equipment. (Examples are telephone switchboards and TV cameras.) When the ancillary equipment is obtained from other sources (indigenous or foreign), the market rationalization involved is accompanied by significant diffusion of technology to the host country.

Corporate Strategy and Technology Transfer

Multinational corporations behave adaptively; they are perhaps the prime example of adaptive behavior among social institutions. The basic strategy of multinational enterprises is to exploit the special circumstances and particular opportunities afforded by operating as a domestic enterprise in each of a number of countries, rather than simply as an importer into those countries. (The difference between these two postures has important legal connotations, particularly as regards "national treatment"; it can also be important to market acceptance and relationships with local industry and financial institutions.) In the pursuit of this strategy they must, of course, adapt to host country laws and government policies, to the peculiar character of the host market and its labor force, and to the international trading position of the host country in the world economy, as well as to those legal constraints and obligations imposed on them by the parent country. These circumstances lead to a dynamic that is basic to the success not only of MNCs but to governments who seek to deal with them in pursuit of the public interest. Just as nations adopt different policies in dealing with MNCs, MNCs adopt different responses to these policies. Comparative advantage is the goal in both instances. Some MNCs rely heavily on centralized planning and control, while others decentralize almost all phases of management and operations. Whatever organizational approach is adopted, success depends heavily on adaptation to local circumstances.

For companies specializing in the manufacture of high-technology products, the scenario for adaptation to a new national market through investment in foreign subsidary usually follows a set pattern.[11]

The first step, taken during the export phase and often before the decision to establish a local subsidiary is made, is to establish a local sales and customer service operation. Customer service—including product application assistance, maintenance, and repair capabilities—is an essential step to significant penetration of a new market for high-technology goods, whether with imported or locally manufactured products. It also represents a first phase in the diffusion of the corporation's unique technology into the host economy. Developing a strong customer service capability is very useful also to the development of local assembly and manufacture, in that it develops a cadre experienced in those skills necessary in production testing and solving production problems.

The second step is the assembly and testing of products from components and subassemblies imported from the parent company. This is followed by the substitution of components from local sources and piece parts fabricated locally for an increasing portion of the imported content. This phase not only increases the local value-added contribution (and thereby decreases import duties) but also permits modest design adaptations to meet the special requirements of the local market (differences in supply voltage, different standards on interconnections, etc.). Success in this phase necessarily requires the development of engineering design capabilities most readily achieved by recruiting local engineers and technicians.

The process just described leads naturally to two important results: a fully integrated manufacturing capability (with its local purchasing and subcontracting elements) and a product development capability combining and exploiting a thorough knowledge of the parent company's relevant technology with a familiarity with host country preferences and requirements. This strategy also minimizes financial risk. The conditions for diffusion of the parent company's technology to the local economy and for the introduction to the broader activities of the MNC of appropriate technology originating in the host country thereby evolve from the MNC's pursuit of its own business interests.

The pace at which the scenario develops is determined primarily by the subsidiary's ability to exploit the opportunities presented by the local market. Other factors enter, of course, including the opportunities for export to third countries and for reimport of the subsidiary's products by the parent company, the accessibility and relative strength of the host country's technological infrastructure, the importance and availability of host government incentive programs for industrial development and export promotion, and so on.

According to an extensive survey of U.S.–based MNCs,[12] the decision to develop a research (as contrasted to a product or process development) program in a foreign subsidiary is largely unrelated to the business scenario described above. Research investment is a part of a long-term business strategy, and any results applicable to immediate product design and sales objectives are regarded as a windfall and not as the justification for basic research. Industrial research is, nonetheless, generally focused in quite specific areas regarded as important to the corporation's long-term development. Corporate managements generally believe that research—more accurately, research scientists—is not "manageable" in the familiar ways (if at all) and that a hands-off approach frequently proves best. Therefore, investment in research (again in contrast to development expenditures) depends critically on access to recognized specialists in the target field and to the specialized facilities required for their effectiveness, and only secondarily on their accessibility to centralized corporate direction. This situation understandably makes corporate managers nervous, oriented as they are to tangible measures of return on investment. Many managements, therefore, determine to bring their research teams together in a central facility where duplication of capital expenditures, at least, is subject to some control and where synergism (a highly regarded concept) has the best hope of bearing fruit. Other managements (those in the pharmaceutical field, for example) tend to invest their research money where the best researchers in a particular field or subspecialty are

Table 4.2
U.S. MNCs: R&D Expenditures at Home and Abroad (1966)

	R&D Expenditures (in millions, except as stated)	Percentage of Total Spent Abroad
Chemicals and drugs	$1.33 billion	6%
Rubber products	131	3
Primary and fabricated metals	322	3
Nonelectrical machinery	833	11
Electrical machinery	1.9	5
Instruments	393	5

SOURCE: *Implications of Multinational Firms for World Trade and Investment and for U.S. Trade and Labor.* Washington, D.C.: U.S. Tariff Commission for the U.S. Senate Committee on Finance, February 1973.

already working. Potential relationships with academic institutions doing pioneering research in fields of special interest are a strong influence in their decision making. The interests that host governments may have in building indigenous research activity are seldom a direct influence on MNC strategy in this regard, although they are a stong indirect influence through their support and encouragement for high-quality independent research institutions.

Taken as a group, U.S.–based high-technology MNCs tend to spend their R&D funds at home. For the research-intensive sectors, the total R&D expenditures of U.S. MNCs and the percentage of this spent abroad are given in Table 4.2. By contrast, MNCs dealing with lumber, wood, and furniture spend 71 percent of their R&D money abroad (but the total spent by U.S. MNCs in this sector was only $86 million in 1966). This is hardly surprising, since the research naturally goes where the trees are and, increasingly, the trees are not in the United States.

MNCs differ from enterprises operating in a single country in a variety of ways. One basic difference is that MNCs must accommodate to the laws, regulations, practices, and political perceptions of a variety of national governments. Because these national environments span a wide range of cultural and societal systems, the challenges to MNC management are manifold.

The national policies of host governments, explicit and implicit, are a strong influence on MNC technology strategies. Since corporate managements of technology-intensive firms would often prefer to export their products from a central operation rather than undergo the risks and the complexities of establishing foreign operations, the corporate decision to create a subsidiary is primarily a response to import tariffs and various nontariff barriers to trade, and to the pattern of government regulations and practices encompassed by the phrase *national treatment*. The principle nontariff barriers affecting high-technology products include: "Buy (Host Country)" preferences, product design and performance standards, and the frequently associated requirement for local testing to demonstrate compliance with such standards. Other government policies also give important advantages to indigenous manufacturers as against importers: government R&D incentives, import substitution and export promotion subsidies, the work permits often required for nonnationals, and the widespread requirement that patents be "worked" locally to remain in force. There are also policies on the part of both host and parent governments that act as disincentives for the creation of subsidiary operations. These include foreign investment constraints, credit restrictions, various regulations (including special tax provisions) regarding the repatriation of earnings and the payment to the parent firm of royalties and management fees.

The MNC must assess and balance each of these factors, as well as a host of related business considerations (e.g., market expectations, return on investment, staffing, intracorporate communications), on a case-by-case basis in arriving at a foreign investment decision. These factors continue to influence succeeding decisions, including those associated with the development of R&D capability in the subsidiary operation. All these factors, therefore, bear on the character and degree of the technology transferred to the host economy through MNCs.

National Technology Strategies and MNCs

MNC operations impinge on many government goals and strategies. To a considerable degree, those concerned with technology are separable from the rest.

Concerns related to balance of payments, maximum employment, and utilization of capital influence governments to maximize the domestic value-added component of their domestic consumption and export of manufactured products. (Of course, this effort must be kept in balance with efforts directed to other important goals, such as freedom of trade.) To this end, governments adopt strategies intended to encourage vertical integration in domestic manufacturing. R&D is seen as an important contributor to this end as well as a source of new products and processes that contribute to economic growth. Creating the conditions that stimulate the development of indigenous R&D capability is thus seen as a desirable end in itself and as a special task for government. The measures customarily adopted can be grouped into three categories:

- Support for scientific and technical education, particularly at the postgraduate level.
- Institution buildings, that is, the creation of research centers independent of, but available to service, individual industrial firms.
- Direct and indirect (e.g., through special tax incentives) support for indigenous R&D in areas viewed as significant to the local economy or to defense needs.

Clearly, policies and government actions in these three areas interact strongly. Research centers and research projects both require an adequate supply of specially trained people. Effective postgraduate S&T training requires close interaction with ongoing research activity. The numbers of individuals receiving advanced technical training and their distribution across the various fields of specialty must be consistent with the absorptive capacity of the research centers and high-technology industry and with current priorities, or a "brain drain" will be inevitable. The policy problems encountered are often intractible, and even a modest degree of success comes hard. It is easy to understand why the responsible government officials often regard industrial enterprises as uncooperative, particularly those firms controlled from abroad.

MNCs have come under particular fire from the developing countries. This matter is dealt with in Chapter 6.

The contributions and the appetites of technology have caused great changes in the scale and composition of world trade, particularly since World War II. The well-known doctrine of comparative advantage provides an economic theoretical base for the clear and rising importance of technology—naked, embodied in products and processes, or implicit in economies of scale and advantages in relative labor productivity—in world trade and investment. Comparative advantage also has brought about the striking growth of multinational corporations in numbers and in economic importance. MNCs, uniquely combining technological know-how, production expertise, and the ability to manage far-flung activity to coherent ends, have become the major vehicle for the international diffusion of industrial technology. This fact has far-reaching implications for public policy, particularly in the areas of national security, development assistance, and supplies of fuels and critical materials. These implications, and the political and technological strategies put forward for dealing with them, are the subjects of the following chapters.

Notes

1. Except as noted, all of the statistical data in this section are from the series *International Economic Report of the President,* prepared annually by the Council on International Economic Policy, Washington, D.C.

2. Johnson, Harry G. *Technology and Economic Interdependence.* New York: St. Martin's, 1975. Chapter 3 provides an excellent summary of the economic theory of technology and trade.

3. Fried, Edward R., and Trezise, Philip H. The United States in the World Economy. In Henry Owen and Charles L. Schultze, eds., *Setting National Priorities: The Next Ten Years.* Washington, D.C.: The Brookings Institution, 1976, p. 80.

4. *Implications of Multinational Firms for World Trade and Investment and for U.S. Trade and Labor.* Washington, D.C.: U.S. Tariff Commission for the U.S. Senate Committee on Finance, February 1973. See also Robert B. Stobaugh, A Summary and Assessment of Research Findings on U.S. International Transactions Involving Technology Transfers. In Rolf R. Piekarz (ed.), *The Effects of International Technology Transfers on the U.S. Economy.* Washington, D.C.: National Science Foundation, 1974.

5. Vernon, Raymond. International Investment and International Trade in the Product Cycle. *Quarterly Journal of Economics,* 1966, **80,** 190–207.

6. Windus, Margaret L., and Schiffel, Dennis D. Recoupment of Government R&D Expenditures: Issues and Practices in the U.S.A. *Research Policy,* 1976, **5,** 180–196.

7. 4,534 Community Multinationals. *Euroforum,* July 13, 1976, Annex 1. Commission of the European Communities, Brussels. See also *Multinational Corporations in World Development.* New York: Economic and Social Council of the UN, 1974.

8. *Implications of Multinational Firms.*

9. *The United States in the Changing World Economy.* Washington, D.C.: Council on International Economic Policy, 1971.

10. Tilton, John E. *International Diffusion of Technology: The Case of Semiconductors.* Washington, D.C.: The Brookings Institution, 1971.

11. Behrman, Jack N., and Wallendar, Harvey W. *Transfers of Manufacturing Technology Within Multinational Enterprises.* Cambridge, Mass.: Ballinger, 1975. An important pioneering collection of case studies.

12. R&D in the Multinational Company. *Managing International Business,* No. 8, New York: National Industrial Conference Board, 1970.

5

TECHNOLOGY AND NATIONAL SECURITY

It is a truism that technology is a principal determinant of military capability and therefore, presumably, of national security. Nuclear and missile technology and undersea technologies have constituted the basis for the strategic balance for at least two decades. Capabilities for tactical warfare have altered enormously also with advances in aviation, communications, electronic sensors, electronic countermeasures, computers, and the technologies of small arms.

Technology, in the form of nuclear weapons and the silent, mindless missiles poised to deliver them, has made obsolete the concept of military superiority, the very notion of military security (if the noun is imputed a literal meaning). Military forces still exist. The Stockholm Institute for Strategic Studies estimated in 1970 that one out of five able-bodied men of working age are under arms throughout the world; the United States and the U.S.S.R. together spend more on their military forces and military largess to their allies than the entire world spends on public education and public health, together. These facts are appalling, but the political reality of military establishments; the undying conviction that sometime, somewhere, war—hopefully limited—may be the only national option; and the grip on official minds of the notion of deterrence all conspire to make the objective examination of how technology contributes to military capability an unavoidable duty. This duty I will discharge, to the best of my ability, in the sections that follow.

One evident result of the impacts of technology on military capabilities has been the dramatic increase since World War II in the proportion of national military budgets that goes to R&D and the associated testing and evaluation of the new products of technology. Other equally important consequences of the central influence of technology on defense planning may not be so obvious. These include:

- The pursuit of R&D strategies that put great emphasis on opportunities for quantum jumps in technological capability. The pursuit of this objective in the context of weapons procurement has led to highly publicized cost overruns and management concentration in the Department of Defense on measures for controlling them.

- Emphasis on weapons standardization among allied groups, particularly NATO and the Warsaw Pact Group, intended to optimize effective cooperation among different national military elements in combat operations and to control the burgeoning cost of weapons systems procurement. The latter concern is a direct consequence of the increased sophistication of military technology. A proposed new military aircraft, the B-1 bomber, was projected to cost $100 million, compared with about $300 thousand for B-17s and B-24s with which the United States fought in World War II. (Taking general inflation into account would reduce this ratio to around 100 to 1!)

- Emphasis on the sale of advanced weapons systems to the nonaligned nations. These programs have strong political and economic motivations, of course, but from the defense standpoint their principal purpose is to amortize the very large costs involved in the development and initial production of new weapon systems as rapidly as possible in order to permit further investment in technology upgrading. Although U.S. military sales to Third World countries were constrained by the Congress in 1976, the United States advanced weapons systems sales to these countries rose from $3.5 billion in 1964 to more than $10 billion in 1977.[1]

- Continued, and perhaps increasing, emphasis on maintaining the secrecy of military technology through classification procedures and strict controls on the export of technology and end items regarded as important to national defense capabilities. This trend is paralleled by increasing emphasis on penetration of the counterpart security of potential adversaries and a rise in expenditures for advanced intelligence-gathering technologies.

The increasing technological sophistication of modern weapons, and the desire of many of our foreign allies to bring to their own civilian economies the spin-off benefits of an active military design and production program, have led to a proliferation of offshore co-production arrangements. These arrangements, which provide for joint participation in the R&D and production phases of new weapons systems, have been undertaken by the United States with France, Japan, the United Kingdom, Germany, Italy, Turkey, and other nations. However, coproduction not only reduces costs to the U.S. taxpayer (a principal objective), it exports jobs. Furthermore, the massive export of the advanced technologies involved increases the likelihood of leaks to potential adversaries, losses that can only be offset by the development of even more advanced weapons systems, at still greater costs. The makings of a vicious circle are apparent.

SECURITY OBJECTIVES FOR TECHNOLOGY

In the never-never land of nuclear strategy, politicians and policy makers debate the merits of "sufficiency" versus those of "superiority." It is time for a philosophical comment. I must emphasize the obvious. Both criteria—sufficiency and superiority—share a basic premise: being "insufficient" or "inferior" is unacceptable. Common wisdom provides support. The necessary logical consequence is that the designated adversary must exhibit the latter qualities. Both cannot be superior; that is obvious. Can both be sufficient? Sufficiency, in the military context, surely implies, as a minimum, the ability to insure that the other side cannot dictate our values and the extent to which we realize them. The philosophical paradox is apparent: If both sides subscribe to the same philosophical dictates, then neither can accept the realization of the other side's end goals. No logical resolution of this paradox is apparent.

Both sufficiency and superiority elude precise definition, which may account for a good deal of the debate. In the technological area the corresponding phrase is *qualitative edge*. Here, in an area where verifiable numbers are the ultimate statement of truth, the definition of the objective is quite openly nonquantifiable. The concept of qualitative superiority has undeniable appeal. We live in a hostile world and with the certain knowledge that superiority in numbers alone—whether numbers of troops, or naval vessels, or missiles, or even of dollars devoted to defense—is no guarantee of survival, let alone winning. Qualitative superiority is our only hope in the event of hostilities and, quite possibly, the basis for deterring hostilities. Furthermore, the notion of qualitative superiority fits comfortably with our image of ourselves as the nation that is best at whatever we turn our efforts to, and certainly best in technology.

The operational difficulty with this formulation of our defense technology policy is that specific choices have to be made. Budgets have to be decided on, including budgets for R&D and for the procurement and deployment of the resulting hardware. Decisions have to be made about military assistance to our allies and to uncommitted nations. Decisions are required in the area of export controls, decisions whether or not to permit exports of particular hardware or technology that might have military applications. All these decisions are necessarily quite specific: explicit identification of priority programs, specific dollar amounts and specific numbers and types of equipment, *yes* and *no* to requests for export licenses covering a particular list of equipment or particular technologies. If nontrivial decisions are required (not simply "zero" or "everything" choices), some manner of quantifying both risk and benefit is necessary. But in fact, such analyses are extremely difficult to make and often hinge on assumptions about the capabilities and intentions of potential adversaries that are impossible to verify.

Defense planners are equally concerned with maintaining the national technological base. Autarky has always been a primary defense objective for all nations. With the increased role of technology in military capabilities, autarky takes on new and difficult dimensions. The indigenous technological capabilities of a large number of nations have increased substantially in recent decades. At the same time, their technological interdependence has increased even more rapidly. This is a reflection not only of increased international trade in the products of technology and the importance to this trade of the activities of high-technology multinational enterprises, but also of increased national specialization in advanced technology represented in the patterns of national concentrations in industry and in research and higher education. The tremendous increase, in the last two decades, in the international mobility of scientists and engineers has also been a major factor in converting what once could be regarded as a firm national technological base to something closer to a structure built on quicksand.

Defense planners have expressed a particular concern with another aspect of the technological base issue that merits a brief discussion, particularly because it arises out of international market competition in high-technology products. For example, the large-scale integrated circuit (LSIC) is of great importance to both industrial and consumer products and to sophisticated military applications. The spectacular penetration of the LSIC into consumer markets (e.g., hand-held calculators and electronic watches) was made possible because the learning curve effect permitted drastic reductions in unit costs with increasing production volumes. With the penetration of these vast markets, LSIC manufacturers found it more profitable to concentrate here than to undertake to design and manufacture (in much smaller quantities) the LSICs needed for military applications. The manufacturers argue that the military needs can be most economically satisfied by using microprocessors, an especially sophisticated form of LSIC that can be programed for a very wide range of different functions.[2] Because of this feature, microprocessors can serve very large consumer markets as well as military markets and thus offer the attractions of learning curve economics. For just this reason, defense planners argue, the international diffusion of microprocessor technology will itself erode U.S. technological superiority.

Efforts to sustain a technological base by concentrating military-related R&D in in-house defense laboratories have, for the most part, proven unsatisfactory. There are probably a number of reasons for this; one of the most important is that in-house R&D groups lack the stimulation of market competition. More than any other factor, it is the stimulus provided by the "innovate or go under" character of the highly volatile, intensely competitive commercial markets in such areas as aviation, electronics, and computers that has accounted for the tremendous dynamism of U.S. technology in these areas since World War II.

THE CASE OF THE COMPUTER

The difficulties involved in objectively assessing the potential adverse impact to U.S. security arising from exports of advanced technology are well illustrated by the case of advanced general-purpose computers. There can be no doubt that the U.S. computer industry enjoys a very large lead over that of the Soviets (who are the standard of comparison in military matters) or that the Soviets are trying very hard to narrow this gap. As of 1970 the United States led the Soviet Union in the number of installed computers (at least ten to one); in computational speed of high-performance production machines (at least 100 to one); in the capacity, access time, and transfer rate of memory units; and in the availability and performance of peripherals, software, and all other elements of computer systems technology. Furthermore, the performance gap (currently five to seven years) has widened steadily for twenty years, and, considering the apparent intractability of Soviet computer production problems and the enormous R&D outlays of the U.S. computer industry (well in excess of $1 billion annually), it may be expected to continue indefinitely.[3]

The Soviet Union is committed at the highest levels to catching up and is devoting very large resources to the effort. In 1973 the Soviets began the introduction of a new computer series, called RYAD, with the goal of producing 12,000 to 15,000 of this series by 1975. (Since 1973 production appeared to be less than 1,000 units, achieving this goal even by 1980 is highly unlikely.) The larger models of the RYAD series copy the features of the IBM 360 series, so the Soviets gain the very important advantages of the ability to use System 360 software and applications programs and any System 360–compatible peripheral equipments they are permitted to import.

There can be no doubt of a computer technology gap, but it must be recognized that the gap itself has no intrinsic importance to U.S. security. What matters is the strategic advantage that might accompany, or arise from, a computer gap.

Advanced general-purpose computers play a significant role in military capability. In addition to their important applications to R&D, general management systems, and the organizations of logistic support, advanced general-purpose computers play an important role in military tasks ranging from nuclear weapons design to computer communications networks. For most such applications existing Soviet production model computers are adequate to maintaining the present strategic balance or, where that might not be true, the Soviet lack of other essential technologies is a more important restraint on their strategic capabilities than the lack of advanced general-purpose computers. This is not to say that greater access to U.S. computer technology would not be advantageous to Soviet military capabilities; only that substantially increased access would not significantly alter the strategic balance in most applications.

However, U.S. willingness to permit the export to the Soviets of such computers could increase the Soviet strategic capabilities, for example, in computer communications systems and ABM systems. Whether this is likely to happen and, if it happened, whether it would have a significant adverse impact on U.S. security are difficult to ascertain. The likelihood that such an adverse impact would occur depends, among other factors, on two determining conditions: Soviet willingness to risk losing the benefits of access to advanced Western computers for essential civilian applications—for instance, production control in truck factories—by diverting systems bought for this agreed purpose to uses unacceptable to the suppliers; and willingness to rely on foreign-manufactured computers for the performance of a central function in an important military capability. (The great differences between the Soviet and U.S. computer industries, especially design approach and production methods and the availability of sophisticated components, essentially rule out the possibility that the purchase of a few models of advanced U.S. systems would offer the Soviets any real opportunity to make significant gains through "reverse engineering," that is, copying.)

Even if an objective analysis were to conclude that the Soviets are willing to accept the risks just cited and thus indicate the possibility of a significant potential security threat, that possibility becomes an actuality only if two further conditions are met. The first is that the Soviets adopt (as a part of their military doctrine and planning) the exploitation of computer communications and ABM systems as a military objective. The fact that the United States has adopted particular objectives does not, per se, demonstrate that these would be in the Soviet interest or consistent with broader Soviet strategic planning. The second condition for the creation of a real security threat is that, presuming the potentials of these technical applications are exploited by the Soviets, the result would adversely impact, in a significant way, on the achievement of U.S. military objectives, either in peacetime or in the event of actual conflict. This is not a foregone conclusion, either.

There are indirect ways the export of U.S. advanced general-purpose computer technology could advance Soviet military capabilities in ways adverse to U.S. interests. The jargon of export control groups these under the rubric of *technology seepage*. The concept of seepage rests on the belief that access to advanced hardware (and the associated operating and maintenance documentation) can permit the buyer to extract critical technical information from visual examination, operation, and testing of the hardware and its components. This is undeniably possible, to some undeterminable degree, when design and manufacturing technology and know-how are involved. In the case of exports involving only end items, technology obtainable in this way is exceedingly limited. Furthermore, such technology as can be gained in this way is necessarily applicable only to new design projects. Therefore, its impact on the capabilities of production machines will be delayed by some years.

Finally, as I pointed out earlier, the basic export control issue here is: Will denial of an export license eliminate, or at least significantly reduce, the adverse effects on U.S. security that might arise if the export were permitted? There are, of course, other sources beyond U.S. control from which the Soviets could obtain advanced general-purpose computers. More fundamentally, there is no evidence that lack of access to imported machines of this type has prevented the Soviets from achieving their priority military objectives. This does not, and logically cannot, mean that there are no military capabilities the Soviets regard as important that they have not already achieved from their own resources. It does mean, however, that we are unable to identify these, if they exist, and that an export control strategy based on the possibility that such situations exist must rest on theoretical, if not purely speculative, reasoning.

It seems to me, on the basis of available analysis, that the United States incurs no significant security hazard in exporting advanced general-purpose computers to the Soviet Union and its allies, providing that two conditions are met. First, the end use should be manifestly "peaceful" and require the fully dedicated capability of the proposed computer system (taking into account reasonable provisions for downtime and workload growth). Second, the fact that the system is indeed dedicated to an approved end-use should be, and remain, reasonably verifiable. Such applications as air traffic control, on-line control of a major production complex, or handling of experimental data generated by a major research facility would seem to fit the first condition; a service bureau function presumably would not. The requirement for verification raises crucial questions, both technical and political, that are harder to settle. The safeguarding of major computer installations as a deterrent to diversion of the system's capability to end uses deleterious to the supplying nation's national security is a complex problem. Inspired initially by the acceptance by most nuclear reactor–exporting countries of the concept of safeguards as a deterrent to proliferation of nuclear weapons (see Chapter 7), the safeguarding of computers has received a great deal of expert study, but the conclusions remain somewhat ambiguous.

To accomplish the deterrent purpose, a computer safeguards system must have two essential characteristics: the ability to detect a diversion and meaningful penalties that can be effectively applied in the event a diversion is detected. Beyond these, an acceptable safeguards system must provide credibility on both sides and with the computer industry, must be administrable, and must not be so expensive as to destroy the economic benefit (to either buyer or seller) of the transaction.

The first of these conditions requires a technique or combination of techniques that will insure an acceptably high probability of detecting a significant diversion combined with a low probability of false alarms. In fact, a very low false alarm rate is even more essential than a very high probability of detection, since false alarms would quickly erode the credibility of the safeguards arrangement, while ordinary prudence will lead the computer user to assume a higher probability of detection than may, in fact, exist. A variety of detection schemes have been proposed, of various levels of sophistication, but the most (and perhaps the only) workable one is frequent, irregular visits to the installation by a U.S. representative well versed in the operation of the computer system. Such visits are virtually mandatory for large installations, in any event, for preventive and corrective maintenance and user training, so little, if any, economic disadvantage is entailed by this approach to safeguarding.

The penalty problem is in some respects as difficult as the detection problem. It is manifestly impracticable to demand the return of the computer system in the event that a serious diversion is detected. (It is literally impossible if the diversion is physical, that is, removal of the equipment to a new and secret location.) A practical penalty measure is the withdrawal of spares and maintenance support, although its effectiveness depends on the degree to which these services and materials may be available to the computer user through other channels, particularly from other installations of the same equipment.

This rather lengthy discussion of computer safeguards is included here not only because of its relevance to the immediate issue, but also because the concept of safeguards has been raised with regard to exports in other high-technology areas. The fundamental requirements and difficulties described here apply equally in those circumstances.

Before leaving the matter of general-purpose computer exports, it is useful to bring out a consideration important to evaluating the potential security impact of all high-technology exports: time delays. When technology flows to a competitor for whom the technology is significantly more advanced than that previously available, it takes time to realize the benefits of the technology acquired. The time delay involved depends on how significantly the new technology differs from the preexisting; for major advances it can run to many years. During the time required to assimilate the new technology, the originator will—if the area of technology has important applications—continue to develop improved technology, and in this process the originator does not suffer the time penalty that is unavoidable for the receiver. In other words, the nation (or, in the commercial context, the firm) that enjoys a large technology lead over its competitors tends to maintain that lead; it is very difficult for the competitor to catch up and almost impossible for it to do so solely by acquiring the leader's technology. In terms of U.S. export control policy, the question of how long it will take the Soviets to capitalize on an imported technology should be weighed against the rate of U.S. technological advance in evaluating the impact of an export on U.S. security.

OTHER EXPORT CONTROL ISSUES

The issues surrounding the export of high-performance general-purpose computers illustrate the generic problems associated with export controls invoked in the name of national security. Computers are a good example of "convertible" technology-based goods; with important, but secondary, alterations in detail design, they are useful to both military and civilian applications. Many other technological products share the same basic character. Integrated circuits make possible the ubiquitous hand-held calculator and are vital to sophisticated missile guidance systems. Advanced machine tools are needed for the efficient production of automobiles and washing machines, and also of tanks and aircraft. Even if it were possible to assure ourselves before permitting an export that its intended application was for peaceful purposes, there is obviously no guarantee that changing circumstances won't alter intentions and no practical means for preventing "forbidden" applications even if we were in a position to determine that they have occurred.

A particular problem in establishing export policies for convertible items relates to component parts, such as integrated circuits. Certain types of components have specific military applicability. Their export can, of course, be prohibited, with varying degrees of confidence that the prohibition will be effective and cannot be circumvented by purchase from other sources. Prohibition of all component exports is clearly impracticable for a variety of reasons (including important political reasons) and might, in fact, be counterproductive in that it would eliminate useful intelligence from analysis of export statistics. Two major questions thus arise, both very difficult to answer with certainty. First, if our adversary has essentially free access to the components required to build computers, radars, or test instruments, for example, how much can the potential hazards to U.S. national security be reduced or contained by prohibiting exports of the equipments themselves? Second, if the components are freely exported, is it reasonable to permit the export of the technology, specialized materials, and unique processing equipment required to manufacture them?

In 1975 the Defense Science Board created a special panel[4] under the chairmanship of Fred Bucy, a well-known industrialist, to reexamine the board problem of controlling exports of military significance. The panel examined in depth those areas of technology—advanced aircraft, instrumentation, semiconductors—recognized as being most sensitive militarily. Specific weapons technologies, such as those used in nuclear weapons or missile guidance, were not considered, since no conceivable security policy would permit their export to potential adversaries; only convertible technologies are at issue. From its examinations and analyses, the Bucy panel drew several conclusions and offered recommendations based on them:

- Technology contained in applied research or development may be of significance for selected areas; but it is "control of design and manufacturing know-how [that] is absolutely vital to the maintenance of U.S. technological superiority. Compared to this, all other considerations are secondary."
- "A new approach to controlling technology exports is overdue. This perspective should focus wholly on technology and not end products of technology. . . ."
- "For the most critical technologies, the U.S. should not release know-how beyond its borders and then depend upon CoCom agreements for absolute control."*

There is, of course, a persuasive logic involved here. It is not the access to a limited amount of sophisticated hardware that creates a military capability but rather the ability to build more of it and to apply the results in advanced weapons systems. Since most of the products of advanced technology do not lend themselves to reverse engineering, that is, the re-creation of a manufacturable design from examination of the finished product, it is the flow of design, and especially production know-how, that must be prevented.† None-

---

*CoCom, the NATO (plus Japan) informal export control coordinating committee, is discussed later in this chapter.

†The East European countries in particular have energetically sought to purchase from the United States and other "Western" nations (including Japan) complete facilities for the production of a variety of sophisticated components—electronic and mechanical—including all of the manufacturing know-how involved and specialized training in its application.

theless, the panel's conclusions and recommendations have been criticized (and as of early 1978 were still "under study" by the Department of Defense). One charge is that they cannot be enforced in practice, particularly those that would curtail the movement of technology to friendly countries, whose attitudes on export controls may be less stringent than ours. A harsher criticism is that controlling the movement of know-how is operationally equivalent to controlling the movements, or at least the activities, of individual Americans and of foreign nationals who may have gained design and production engineering experience through study in U.S. universities or employment with U.S. firms. Nothing short of a police state could enforce the panel's proposals, some have charged.

The problem of policy controls on the export of convertible technologies, whether embodied in process or end product, remains. The issues involved in each case are extremely difficult to resolve on the basis of objective analysis. Since the economic stakes are high, potential exporters will understandably press hard for approval. The security interests of the nation must be put ahead of the commercial interests of any firms or industry, but government intervention in trade is justified only when objective analysis shows the nation's interests to be threatened. Clearly judgment is entailed, and equally qualified and thoughtful people will often arrive at different conclusions.

Institutional Problems in Export Control

Not surprisingly, the substantive difficulties surrounding governmental intervention in international trade for national security reasons described above are greatly compounded by a variety of intractable institutional problems. The institutional arrangements, domestic and international, reflect in their complexity the obvious fact that many legitimate national interests (and the corresponding governmental and nongovernmental constituencies) are affected. When this is the case, it is inevitably true that the working of the institutional arrangements will be characterized by conflicts of intentions.

The way the U.S. government organizes itself to deal with the export of advanced technology depends largely on the case in question. Frequently, major technology export issues are exceedingly complex, with multiple variables and trade-offs involving security, foreign policy, and economic interests. It is difficult if not impossible to force meaningful technology export policy decisions on a hypothetical basis. In general, it takes the confrontation of an actual case to produce a firm policy position.

In the U.S. government four agencies currently share major responsibility for licensing the export of hardware and technical data. The Department of State, in consultation with the Department of Defense, has jurisdiction over licensing U.S. industry export of arms, ammunition, implements of war (including space items), and the data and technology that relate directly to such articles. The principal legal basis for this jurisdiction is contained in the International Traffic in Arms Regulations and the Mutual Security Act of 1954, as amended.

The Department of State also has policy responsibilities for certain other types of exports under the Mutual Defense Assistance Control Act of 1951 (Battle Act). State also represents the United States in the CoCom, a multilateral organization involving the United States, the NATO allies (except Iceland), and Japan in the control of exports to the socialist bloc. Export control procedures relating to military equipment and technology and to security assistance programs are handled by the Department of Defense.

The Nuclear Regulatory Commission has statutory responsibility for controlling the export of nuclear materials and technical data (See Chapter 7).

The Department of Commerce is the major U.S. agency involved in export licensing and control programs. Commerce has the responsibility for licensing those commodities and technical data that are not classified and not the responsibility of the Department of State or the Nuclear Regulatory Commission.

The original establishment of export controls was motivated primarily by foreign policy and national security considerations and the need to create a framework whereby the outflow of military-related products and technology could be regulated. While military and strategic considerations continue to be the predominant influence in the export licensing decisions, economic and commercial considerations also enter into the decision-making process.

For example, Section 414 of the Mutual Security Act of 1954 authorizes the regulation of export of items on the Munitions List (established by that act) and related technical data "in furtherance of world peace and the security and foreign policy of the U.S." The Department of State regards economic-commercial factors as integral to U.S. foreign policy within the meaning of the Mutual Security Act. In Munitions List cases that have important economic-commercial ramifications, the State Department seeks advice and guidance from other government agencies, such as the Treasury and the Department of Commerce. Advice from White House staff sources is also sought, particularly the National Security Council.

While the Export Control Act of 1949 and its successor legislative authority (the Export Administration Act of 1960, as amended*) authorized the imposition of export controls to protect the U.S. domestic economy from the excessive drain of scarce materials and to further the foreign policy interests and international responsibilities of the United States, in recent years the principal purpose of the act has been to control those exports that might adversely affect U.S. national security interests. (From time to time, controls on various basic commodities and foodstuffs have been invoked under this legislation.) As such, most of its control efforts have been directed against the Soviet Union, other East European and Asian communist countries, and Cuba. In determining whether prospective exporters are to be granted licenses (in those cases where a formal validated license is required), the responsible office is not influenced by the fact that the U.S. government may have contributed financially to the development of the product or technology. Moreover, in replacing the Export Control Act of 1949 with the Export Administration Act of 1969, Congress removed the phrase "export makes a significant contribution to the . . . economic potential of such nation or nations . . .," which had earlier established one criterion for granting a license to a proposed export. This modification reflected Congressional feeling that the possibility that the export would strengthen the economy of the receiving nation was not of itself contrary to the security or foreign policy interests of the United States. In fact, a subsequent amendment to the 1969 act added language asserting that "it is the policy of the Government to encourage the widest possible range of exports, including technical data, for peaceful purposes."

The recent history of export control legislation amply illustrates a familiar policy dilemma: the Congress seeks to serve two goals— national security and maximum export earnings—that conflict in a basic way. At the same time that recent legislation has been loaded with a variety of "sales promotion" provisions, the security dimension has been tightened further. In 1976 Senators Jackson and Cranston succeeded in introducing amendments that gave the Department of Defense an effective veto power on any export. Early versions of the 1977 bill would have required, in the extreme case,

---

*The act expired in 1976 without renewal but controls were continued unchanged under an executive order. As of late 1977 passage of new legislation awaited resolution of Congressional differences regarding the handling of the Arab boycott of U.S. firms doing business with Israel.

universities offering engineering curricula to nationals from countries to which exports are controlled to report the details to the Secretary of Commerce. (In a fit of second thought this provision was watered down.)

International Problems

It was pointed out earlier that the NATO allies (plus Japan) have organized an international consultative mechanism (CoCom) to concert their respective approaches to controlling the export of potentially strategic goods and technology to the socialist bloc countries. It is important here to point out some of the differences in national perspectives regarding trade and security that increasingly encumber it.

In the first place, national governments quite understandably have differing views of what constitutes a strategic export, reflecting their differing geopolitical environments and conceptions of strategy, as well as their own approaches to weapons systems planning and development (which each national defense establishment tends to project onto the strategy and tactics of potential adversaries).* A consolidated CoCom list of embargoed items exists, but the United States, for example, carries many additional items on its control listings. Secondly, the participating governments have quite different views of urgency of the threat to their national security posed by the intentions and tactics of perceived potential adversaries. These understandable differences lead directly to differing views on the treatment of particular export licensing decisions. Finally, each of the participating nations has strong economic incentives to increase its export trade. In pursuit of the goal of comparative advantage, each seeks the maximum flexibility for exports in those technological areas in which it has the greatest relative strength. Because of the obvious disparities and asymmetries that exist among the trading nations in this respect, the representatives to CoCom from the different countries pursue differing objectives, both as regards what it is appropriate to export and (equally important from the standpoint of commercial competition) what should not be permitted as exports from other participants.

---

*In commenting editorially on the weapons planning of NATO, Robert Hotz—who is widely quoted by "hard liners" on security matters—said, "Western observers tend to misinterpret Soviet requirements and goals in terms of our own" (*Aviation Week*, November 1, 1976).

Under these circumstances the collective judgment of CoCom tends always toward export approval for those items the majority of members seek to sell, responding always to national judgments regarding the proper balance between economic and security interests. CoCom is a rather elderly undertaking, as such organizations go, and its effective functioning is not the highest priority concern of the political leadership of any of the participating governments. Competitive pursuit of detente is certain to erode its effectiveness even more deeply. It is unlikely that the erosive trend will be arrested, barring some development in international politics that re-creates the kind of collective political will that gave it birth.

Weapons Sales and Technology Flows

Sales of advanced weapons systems, often embodying the latest technologies, are made to both allies and nonallies. World arms orders exceeded $20 billion in 1976, about half to be supplied by the United States, with about two-thirds of the total going to nations classified as developing.[5] The great bulk of the orders are for technologically-sophisticated items. There are important foreign policy objectives affected by U.S. participation in this worldwide traffic in arms, but the following discussion is focused on the implications of the technology transfers involved for national security.

The United States is usually the preferred supplier of arms, particularly because we have shown an exceptional willingness to provide spare parts support and intensive training of customer nationals in operation, maintenance, and repair. In many instances, the United States has agreed to coproduction of major subcomponents of the systems involved—arrangements where the foreign purchaser is provided the technology, detailed manufacturing data, and specialized training to produce essential subassemblies for its own use and for incorporation in U.S. production. Such arrangements are standard with the NATO allies and Japan, but they have been extended on occasion to such nations as Spain, Israel, Taiwan, South Korea, and Iran. As of the end of 1976, resistance to such arrangements, from organized labor, the U.S. supplying firms, and even the Department of State, seemed to be on the rise.[6] Buyer pressures for such arrangements are rising also, not only because of the hard-currency savings that result but also because coproduction arrangements necessarily transfer technological know-how that might be put to use in support of the broader economic development objectives of the foreign partner nation.

These arms sales, and the coproduction arrangements that accompany them, are welcomed by Department of Defense officials because they reduce the unit costs of the systems to the DOD budget. The total impact, however, is not as clearly positive. As Gelb points out, "by selling some of its most sophisticated weaponry, the U.S. was losing technological superiority over other forces and running the risk of the technology falling into hostile hands. . . . The Soviet Union, to be sure, was running into similar problems."[7] The result for both superpowers, therefore, is accelerated technological obsolescence of the respective defense capabilities, necessitating still greater investments in weapons R&D and prototype procurement. Arming the nonaligned, then, is a dubious contribution to mutual deterrence and a powerful incentive to still greater commitments to sustaining the arms race.

The arms trade situation has attracted the attention of both the Congress and President Carter. The International Security Assistance and Arms Export Control Act of 1976 states, "It shall be the policy of the U.S. to exert leadership in the world community to bring about arrangements for reducing the international trade in implements of war. . ." and calls on the president to initiate multilateral discussions for that purpose. In a May 1977 press conference President Carter announced as policy that "the U.S. will henceforth view arms transfers as an *exceptional* foreign policy instrument" (emphasis added) and that "the burden of persuasion will be on those who favor a particular arms sale, rather than those who oppose it." The President announced that the United States would begin talks soon with the Soviet Union, the United Kingdom, France, and West Germany (the other major weapons suppliers) on measures for multilateral action. The new policy also prohibited coproduction agreements for "significant weapons, equipment and major components." The last element represents a major policy change, and one that is likely to impact strongly on U.S. relationships with NATO, particularly as regards weapons standardization.

The maintenance of a military capability adequate to contain perceived threats is a proper—indeed, essential—goal for every government. In today's world military capability is intimately tied to technology in the design and production of advanced weapons and in the infrastructure that supports their deployment. In this area, then, technological advance—invention and innovation—is destabilizing. Since a very wide range of technological innovations are convertible to either military or civil use, efforts to constrain the world arms race by prohibiting R&D in particular areas are doomed to failure. The family of nations must pursue other avenues of policy development if the awful threat of war is to be contained.

Notes

1. These data and those of the following paragraphs, collected from a variety of sources, are presented together with a thoughtful analysis of their significance to U.S. foreign policy in Leslie H. Gelb, Arms Sales. *Foreign Policy*, Winter 1976–1977, 3ff. See also *World Military Expenditures and Arms Trade, 1963–1973*. Washington, D.C.: U.S. Arms Control and Disarmament Agency, 1975, and subsequent documents in this series.
2. Lockerd, R.M. Electronic Technology Progress and Life Cycle Support. *Defense Systems Managment Review*, 1977, **1**, 2.
3. Berenyi, Ivan. Computers in Eastern Europe. *Scientific American*, 1970, **223**, 4.
4. *An Analysis of Export Control of U.S. Technology: A DOD Perspective*. Washington, D.C.: Defense Science Board, Task Force on Export of U.S. Technology, 1976.
5. Gelb, Arms Sales.
6. Baranson, Jack. Technology Exports Can Hurt Us. *Foreign Policy*, Winter 1976–1977, **25**, 180ff.
7. Gelb, Arms Sales, p. 8.

6

TECHNOLOGY
AND DEVELOPMENT

EMERGENCE OF THE LESS DEVELOPED
COUNTRIES

The end of World War II left a world suffering from profound dislocations in many areas. Not only were the socioeconomic structures of most of Europe, Japan, China, the Soviet Union, and most of South Asia in ruins, but the colonial ties that had bound much of Africa and Asia to Europe and Japan were broken, or about to be. Within fifteen years over sixty new nations gained formal independence. Independence brought a new political consciousness, particularly when these new countries assumed membership in the United Nations and discovered the potentials of one nation-one vote politics. Independence also carried with it a backlog of deep poverty and only the vaguest comprehension of the complexities of self-government.

It was inevitable that the new superpowers, the United States and the U.S.S.R., should have seen in the newly emerging nations both threat and opportunity: the threat of political alignment with the other side and the opportunity to shape the policies and economies of the new states to their own image. The new nations clearly needed help—how badly no one yet appreciated—and the superpowers entered into competition in providing it. Seeing the help offered by the Soviets as subversive to both free world interests and those of the "legitimate" governments of the new states, President Truman in 1949 announced the Point Four program, and formal U.S. assistance to the less developed world was born.

DEFINITIONS OF *LESS DEVELOPED*

What does *less developed* mean? Originally the term was seen largely in terms of political sophistication; development was loosely equated with a strong and stable central government. Economic problems were recognized, of course, but it was generally assumed (by both the United States and the U.S.S.R.) that these would be dealt with internally if the "right" governments could be established. The broader dimensions of the problems of development became clear very soon. Level of development can be measured in many ways: GNP per capita; industrial output; extent of illiteracy; unemployment and underemployment; proportion of the population living outside the money economy; rate of fixed capital formation; and so on.*

Nations differ widely in these respects as in others, of course, so that less developed by no means implies a homogenous group of economically underprivileged countries. The United Arab Emirates, for example, which would qualify as less developed by almost every other test, earn from their petroleum exports annual revenues that push their GNP per capita to above $11,000 per year, higher than that of any other nation. The Emirates and the other smaller nations whose buried treasures of petroleum or minerals essential to modern industry have so far done little for the lives of most of their populations face special problems of development and must be considered separately from the resource-poor, generally overpopulated nations that comprise most of the less developed world. I will discuss these special problems later in this chapter.

Less developed is a characterization obviously applicable not only to nations. The Eskimos and dozens of other similar cultural, ethnic, and regional groups are even less developed than the average citizen of the poorest nations, but it is not conventional to think of the problems of development in this way. This points up a feature of less developed nations that is important to international politics.

---

*The UN statistical organization has adopted GNP per capita as the basis for its definition of development. Using $200 as the threshold, the Development Assistance Committee of OECD has estimated that in 1973, 54 percent of the world population resided in countries thus defined as less developed.

Less developed countries, in addition to qualifying under one or more of the statistical measures cited, are often characterized also by a high degree of political visibility: Their citizens (at least influential segments of them) reflect their desires for improvement of their socioeconomic condition in intense and often radical political activism, and their governmental leaders are equally active in their insistence on international acceptance of their political objectives and, frequently, of international responsibility for solving their problems.

The less developed countries that are the generally accepted beneficiaries of development assistance, whatever their statistical descriptors, have four features in common:

- A wide and usually widening gap between the actual standard of living and the conscious aspirations of their people.
- A narrow economic base. Their societies and economies are, for the most part, static, predominantly agricultural, and dependent for foreign currency earnings on the export of one or two staple commodities, sometimes augmented with simple manufactured goods that cannot command a high profitability.
- A chronic shortage of indigenous investment capital.
- All of the above factors reinforced by a low level of general education and technical training, a shortage of entrepreneurs, and a general lack of economically exploitable skills.

The very existence of the less developed countries (we will call them LDCs, for short) and the political, social, and economic tensions they create among the community of nations make the problem of dealing with them a central concern of the foreign policy of each of the advanced nations, particularly the United States. Our national awareness of these problems has been heightened in the very recent past by the recognition that we and our principal allies and trading partners are, as a group, almost totally dependent on the LDCs for the fuels and raw materials critical to our standard of living, and we rely on them also as markets for the exports essential to paying our fuel bills. (In 1975, 37 percent of U.S. exports of manufactured goods went to LDCs.[1]) We watch with ever-increasing anxiety the widening gaps—social, economic, and political—between ourselves and the LDCs and among the diverse groups of LDCs themselves. Belatedly recognizing the global interdependence that has characterized much of the world since colonial and even precolonial times, we are painfully aware of the need to do something to arrest and reverse the growing and threatening divisiveness among us. The most familiar political instrument at hand is development assistance.

DEVELOPMENT ASSISTANCE

In the early post–World War II period, development assistance largely took the form of security assistance, that is, supplying the arms that "legitimate" governments needed to keep their political opposition under control. This approach was rather quickly supplemented by food aid when it became apparent that widespread hunger was a driving factor in the internal political instability of the less developed countries. When this combination failed to yield the desired results, the United States and the other advanced nations (who have followed an almost identical strategy throughout) added capital assistance. At first the results appeared to be encouraging. Between 1950 and 1967 the LCDs as a group increased their GNP by an average annual rate of 4.8 percent; a rate considerably faster than that at which the advanced countries grew in earlier stages of their development. Much of the gain, unfortunately, was absorbed by the accelerating rate of LDC population growth, so that average growth in per capita GNP was no more than 2 or 2.5 percent.[2] The president of the World Bank has forecast that the poorest LDCs (those with current per capita annual income under $200) will embrace a total population of 1 billion by 1980 and will realize a growth in per capita income of only 0.2 percent annually from 1970 to 1980.[3] Low economic growth rate is in itself comparable with the early experience of the advanced countries, but that simple measure obscures rather than illuminates the real picture. In fact, income disparity between the tiny rich and middle classes in these countries and that realized by the mass of the poor increased rather than diminished. According to the UN Food and Agriculture Organization (FAO), after two decades of development assistance the average person in the least developed countries was more poorly fed in 1975 than in 1950. Perhaps three-quarters of the population of the LDCs live, even now, on a subsistence basis, entirely outside the money economy and totally untouched by billions of dollars in capital assistance.

Beginning in the mid-1960s, the attention of those concerned with aid to the LDCs shifted from capital assistance to technical assistance. Only if the continually increasing populations of the LDCs could learn to make do for themselves—through the substitution of modern technologies for the primitive methods that characterize their agriculture, their cottage industries, and, in fact, every aspect of their economic lives—could they hope to narrow the development gap and could we hope to be relieved of the growing burdens of capital charity. This new perspective led to, and in turn was reinforced by, the United Nations Conference on the Application of Science and Technology for the Benefit of the Less Developed Areas (UNCSAT), held in 1963. At this conference 1,665 participants from 96 nations and 108 international agencies produced eight volumes of reports but, in the end, little action, national or international. The UN secretariat undertook follow-through responsibilities that culminated in 1971 in publication of the World Plan of Action,[4] produced by a new Advisory Committee on the Application of Science and Technology to Development (ACAST) established by the Economic and Social Council.

Technology has an obvious relevance to almost every sector of modern society: to agriculture and fishing, to mining, to the exploitation of forest products, to industrial production and distribution, to provision of fuels and all forms of energy. Technology also has obvious roles throughout the social infrastructure: in education, health care, public safety and defense; in communications and transportation; and in the preservation of the cultural heritage. It would seem to be a safe premise, therefore, that technology is relevant to the LDCs; that, in fact, it is their inability to employ modern technology in all of these areas that accounts for their poverty and backwardness. Give them technology and they will join the modern world, to their unarguable benefit. However, this may not be true, and, even if true, it may not be possible.

It does not make one a racist or a believer in genetically imposed limitations to question the notion that technology as it is known and understood in the advanced industrial nations is relevant to the needs and aspirations of all nations, or that, whatever their traditional beliefs and values, the LDCs would contribute to world peace and harmony if they "got on with the job of catching up." Even if such iconoclastic views were proved to be indefensible, there still remains the question of whether the mastery of modern technology is enough. Is technological capability a sufficient condition for a nation's success, assuming that it is a necessary condition? History has yet to provide an unequivocal answer.

The geopolitical forces that define national boundaries have behaved in an arbitrary, sometimes whimsical, fashion. Nonetheless, the societal differences among nations are profound. Perhaps the very notion of national identity requires such differences. In any event, the historic pervasiveness of international conflict should be adequate proof of national differences.

It is a common conceit to picture the differences between the LDCs and the advanced industrial nations in terms of "time frame." Time "moves more slowly" for the LDCs, or they "belong to the Middle Ages." The notion is absurd. Time has its meaning in human terms, in the processes of personal maturity and the inexorable march of generations; it is not fixed by external events. Time is a commodity more precious to and less available to the LDCs than to the advanced nations, but need doesn't determine reality. The time reference approach has a more particular shortcoming in the context of technical assistance to development. If one views the challenge of development as a collapsing of the time dimension—a kind of quick-tempo bypassing of the *andante* pace of the Industrial Revolution—one misconstrues the problem. To the extent that the pace of the spread of the Industrial Revolution to what have become the advanced nations was set by the availability of technology (and more particularly by the intellectual concepts and societal structures that together provide desired technology), the historical situation is not relevant to the present circumstances of the LDCs. On the other hand, to the extent that a society's technological resources are a reflection rather than a determinant of its culture in a broad sense, the cultural affinities of the LDCs may not encourage the acceptance of, let alone the generation of, technological stimulants to "progress."

If the concept of compressing the time scale is not an adequate descriptor of the technological needs and aspirations of the LDCs, what other concept is valid? The answer is not obvious. Perhaps it will be suggested by a more detailed examination of the problem.

The basic problem of national development is a circular one. An obvious starting point is the need for the skills (at all levels and of all kinds) required to assimilate and exploit technology and the lack of the institutional structures to harness those skills effectively (itself a consequence of lack of skills, among other factors). The development of technical skills requires education and experience. The development of infrastructure implies an accepted social goal and the human, material, and political resources necessary to its accomplishment. Investment in education is justified by an outlet for its product. Both education and infrastructure require capitalization and, ultimately, the income to sustain it. Capitalization is induced by

the preexistence of the skills and institutions necessary to its suste-
nance and growth. And so we are back at the beginning.

The choice of a strategy for development is obviously important.
Before a logical choice of strategy can be made, however, it is necessary to define the goals sought and to examine the obstacles in the
way of their achievement. Removing or circumventing these obstacles may not prove to be an adequate initiator for development;
there is no assurance that releasing the brakes on the societal vehicle
will automatically result in its accelerating in the desired direction,
but removing the brakes would seem to be a necessary starting condition.

Goals and Requirements of Development

Defining the goals of the development process has been the subject
of much rhetoric and a significant amount of thoughtful analysis.
There is little agreement. The leaders of the developing and those of
the advanced countries address the question from different perspectives, and both groups not infrequently betray an understandable
chauvinism. In the absence of consensus, I will provide my own
definition of these goals:

- To obtain an adequate standard of living for each citizen. (Let
  adequate remain without precise definition; the objective is sound
  on any basis: humanitarian, sociological, political.)
- To balance population growth with growth in means, leaving
  some margin for improvements in the quality of life.
- To develop the societal infrastructure that is a prerequisite to viable nationhood—effective government without repression, mass
  communication (in the broadest sense), an educational system
  adequately serving both the nation and the individual, the essen-
  tials of public health and safety, a political system that can resist
  aggression from within or without.
- To eradicate disabling disease, eliminate illiteracy, contain crime,
  and live in peace with neighboring states.
- To create for every citizen a sense of national identity and of participation in national life, political and economic. [5]

This is heady stuff, some of it beyond the demonstrated capacities
of even the most developed nations. Can any nation, formulating its
goals, settle for less?

The requirements for development are, properly, stated in more pragmatic terms:

- Bringing the productivity of labor and the return on capital to a "positive feedback" level, that is, to the point where the economic value of the output sufficiently exceeds the total costs of input so that a surplus is generated, which can be reinvested to obtain still larger surpluses and qualitative social gains. A society incapable of producing above the subsistence level can never develop, economically or in any other meaningful sense.
- A pattern of social distribution of material benefit that creates stakeholders in the development process in the laboring class, the middle class, and among civil servants, not simply among the already wealthy. (In many LDCs the very wealthy have nothing important to gain and much to risk from the pursuit of national development.)
- Reduction of unemployment to the point where its social cost can be borne by the employed without sacrifice of the potential for growth—quantitative and qualitative—and its maintenance there.
- A balance of international trade; necessary to a viable money economy and to creation of an environment that attracts the infusion of capital from abroad.
- The possibility of upward social mobility; essential to the development of an entrepreneurial class and to continued evolution of the social infrastructure.
- Stabilization of the "brain drain." Some emigration from the intellectual class is, in all likelihood, an unavoidable marginal cost of access to the specialized opportunities for training abroad that are essential to certain aspects of development. Too large a "brain drain" is clear evidence of a societal disequilibrium, which, if it persists, will levy heavy penalties on the rate of development.
- A societal infrastructure that develops at a rate that keeps pace with other aspects of development, never lagging so far as to put a brake on the positive elements of the development process but never leading so far as to create a gulf between aspiration and achievement leading to disabling frustration and despair.
- A "kicker." If the development process is ever to get off the ground and to gain momenturm, some essential ingredient must be sufficiently in surplus and sufficiently exploitable to permit, temporarily, its substitution for other essential ingredients that may be missing or have not achieved "critical mass." The kicker

might take several forms: an abundant natural resource that can serve a world market need, a substantial infusion of foreign capital, a particularly gifted political leadership. The kicker function cannot be relied on indefinitely. Development will go off the tracks, or grind to a halt, unless all the resource elements—economic, material, human—can be brought into balance at levels that will insure their continued and increasing availability.

Technology clearly plays essential roles in the development process. Suitably selected, adapted, and exploited, it provides the means for increased labor productivity and return on capital. It is crucial to almost every aspect of the social infrastructure, from highways and telecommunications to abundant energy at acceptable cost, from equitable and efficient tax collection to public health and safety, from classroom materials to newspapers. Technology is essential to adequate supplies of food and water and the safe disposal of wastes. Technology is needed to displace imports and create exports. Technology provides the necessary vehicle for the emergence of an entrepreneurial class.

Appropriate Technologies

Development needs *appropriate* technologies. The statement is so self-evident as to sound trivial. However, defining, locating, choosing, and acquiring appropriate technologies turns out to be a profoundly challenging task.[6] Often, the technologies appropriate to development are not those employed in the more advanced countries.

What constitutes appropriate technology for development? The general answer, of course, is technology appropriate to the context—appropriate to the objectives, resources, and opportunities of the developing countries. Since these factors are unique to each country and to each point in its development, the judgment as to which technologies are appropriate is unique to place and time. What is appropriate in one context may prove singularly inappropriate in another. The criteria by which appropriateness can be measured, however, can be generalized with some assurance:

- *Scale.* The utility of almost any form of technology depends, among other factors, on the intended scale of its use. Hoes are appropriate to kitchen gardens; tractor-drawn gang plows are appropriate to the wheatfields of the Dakotas. Numerically controlled multiple-spindle boring mills are appropriate to the Detroit automobile manufacturers; handcranked drill presses are appropriate to the blacksmith shops of Bangladesh.

- *Skills.* The technology employed must be appropriate to the levels of training and skills of both the producers and the ultimate users of a product and to the people engaged in the necessary distribution and servicing arrangements. The cheap labor characteristic of LDCs is an advantage only to the extent that the technology chosen exploits the highest available skills of the labor force.

- *Materials.* The technology must be adapted to locally available raw and semifinished materials and components (e.g., minor hardware items), taking into account the prevailing quality, uniformity, and costs of these items. The energy required to exploit the technology must be available at acceptable costs and in assured supply.

- *Physical Environment.* The technology must be appropriate to physical environment: temperatures, humidity, and salinity of the atmosphere; character of the soil; availability of water; presence of destructive insects and rodents; pervasiveness of blowing sand and dust; and so forth.

- *Cultural Affinities.* The end product must be acceptable to the intended users in light of their traditions and taboos. (It is on this score that many well-meaning efforts to introduce new food technologies to the LDCs have foundered.)

- *Management.* The skills and experience required to manage all aspects of the technological enterprise must be available and usable in light of local customs and traditions.

- *Capital Costs.* The capital required to employ effectively a particular technology must be available at a cost commensurate with the economic benefits provided by the technology and competitive with other opportunities for investment. Generally, for a technology to be appropriate to the resource-poor LDCs, its capital-intensity must be low.

These requisites apply to all forms of technology, though they may have quite different implications in different economic sectors and different national circumstances.

It is implicit in the above list that the proper technologies for development will generally not be those in wide use in the more advanced countries. This is a reflection of major differences not only in the relative costs of the factors of production—labor, materials, and capital—but also in patterns of consumption. Much of the technology of the advanced countries is employed to satisfy the tastes of a large and relatively affluent middle class and is thus irrelevant to the development of the LDCs.

The disparities between technologies appropriate to the United States and those appropriate to particular LDCs can be illustrated adequately by a single example, agriculture. In the United States, where exceptional natural endowments of fertile soil and good growing weather combine with the exploitation of a wide range of sophisticated technologies to yield the highest agricultural productivity in the world, the average number of (full-time equivalent) farm workers per 100 acres in fewer than 0.5. In Mexico the corresponding number is 12, and in Taiwan it is 71.[7] This clearly demonstrates that agricultural technology that has proved successful in the United States is inappropriate to many of the developing countries on the basis of scale alone. It may also be inappropriate in regard to other requisites listed, particularly skills, physical environment, and capital cost.

Appropriate technology need not and should not mean primitive technology, even for the poorest countries. Providing that it meets the requisites listed earlier, the best available technology is appropriate. *Best,* in this regard, doesn't mean most complicated. The best technology is that which performs the intended function most effectively and reliably and at the lowest acceptable cost. Its application entails careful design, appropriate use of available materials and production capabilities, and thoughtful attention to user needs and preferences. The best technology eliminates unnecessary frills and complexity, provides for long and dependable service life, and minimizes operating cost. Examples of best technologies that have a place in the development process include high-yield and pest- and disease-resistant seeds, birth control pills, and rotary tilling machines.

Under proper conditions very advanced technologies can serve important development needs. *Proper conditions,* in this context, implies the conjunction of a specific and visible need, an appropriate technological means for meeting the need, and the political will on the part of government officials and technological leaders to commit themselves to success. The AID Aid Sat project of 1976 provides a good demonstration of what can be done. Using air transportable ground terminals with the NASA Advanced Technology Satellite (ATS-6), an AID team demonstrated the potential applications of satellite communications, satellite earth resource surveys, and satellite data for disaster prediction and relief planning in twenty-seven LDCs. The response was very positive, and the AID budget for support of this program was increased by seven times in one year.

Technology Transfer

The political leaders of the advanced countries reaffirm on frequent and generally well-publicized occasions their unalterable commitment to the transfer of (appropriate) technology to the developing countries. The political leaders of the developing countries as frequently, and generally with greater passion, reaffirm their conviction that the promised technology transfer doesn't happen, or doesn't work out, or serves only the interests of the "economic colonialists" at the expense of the needs of the developing countries. The conflict is more than rhetorical (although there is much of that on both sides). It reflects basic differences in perception of the purpose of technology transfer for development, differences in judgments about the value of what actually transpires, and the intrinsic difficulties that surround the process.

The difficulties that arise in the transfer of technology for development take several forms. Recognizing the developing countries' needs for appropriate technology and accepting the sincerity of the advanced countries' professions of their desire to meet these needs, several questions must be addressed:

Where does the appropriate technology come from? Except for the socialist bloc nations (whose technologies have proven to be at least as inappropriate to the needs of development as those generated in the West), most of the relevant hard technology is the property of industrial firms. Government may have a "free right of use" to some of it, arising from the provisions of government contracts that contributed to its development, but a right of use doesn't imply either a right to permit others to use (except as agents of the "owner" government) or, more importantly, possession of the skills and experience necessary to using it. The government can and does hold rights to inventions (the U.S. government holds title to more than 20,000 patents), but the ownership of a patent doesn't require or imply the ability to exploit it effectively for practical purposes.* Private ownership of a technology represents, in all countries, a recognized property right. Its use by another creates a legal right to fair compensation to the owner, a right that governments cannot abridge. Furthermore, private ownership of a technology, particularly by a commercial enter-

---

* It is worth noting the fact (startling in the light of the frequency with which technical assistance proposals based on a total misunderstanding in this respect are put forward) that of the total number of patents owned by the U.S. government, only a trivial proportion—on the order of 1 percent—have been filed in any foreign country. Since, under the usual provisions of foreign patent laws, the grant of a U.S. patent constitutes publication of its content and prior publication precludes the granting of a patent, U.S. patents not filed in foreign countries within one year of U.S. filing are in the public domain in those countries and as such are available for free exploitation within those countries by anyone.

prise, implies that its realization in practical terms reflects the particular capabilities of that enterprise and the special characteristics of the market served by it. The technology may hold promise of realization in a form appropriate to other circumstances, but this adaptation won't occur in the absence of a viable and accessible market reflecting those circumstances.

Who will identify appropriate technologies? (This important question could equally well be phrased *who can?*) The operative words are *who* and *appropriate*. Appropriate is a judgmental measure; its successful application requires a clear and pragmatic understanding of needs and circumstances as well as what is entailed in implementing a technology successfully, a kind of understanding that derives only from responsible experience in an enterprise devoted to the exploitation of technology. As much as any other factor, the need for development reflects the shortage of individuals who combine these kinds of know-how. Technological entrepreneurs abound in advanced countries, but they know too little about the special needs and circumstances of the developing countries to be particularly helpful to the identification process. Technically trained people exist in the developing countries—indeed they are sometimes in oversupply—but though they may understand very well the needs and circumstances of their national environment, very few of them have any working knowledge of the strategies, skills, and practices involved in the successful exploitation of technological know-how for practical market-satisfying purposes.

Once an appropriate technology is identified, how is it acquired and exploited? There are a variety of legitimate means. It may be obtained as an outright gift, it can be purchased, it can be licensed, it can be the subject of a joint venture, or those who own it can be invited (or induced through various concessional measures) to put it to work in a developing economy in their own commercial interests. The viability of each of these possibilities is limited by the prevailing circumstances and by the inducements offered by the would-be acquirer. The inducements may be purely political or purely economic, or they may involve a combination of both. In any event, a negotiation is involved, which implies that both sides have something to offer, something they desire, and the skill and patience to find a viable linkage.

How does the developing country pay for acquired technology? Technology is an asset for those who control it. Those who wish to acquire it tacitly acknowledge this by the fact of their interest in it. Which other assets available to the would-be acquirer and desired by the owner can be exchanged for the technology in question? The most obvious, most fungible, and frequently least available in developing countries is money (especially as foreign exchange). In lieu of money other tangible assets may be used, particularly raw materials. Intangible assets may be even more convertible in such transactions; for instance, market access or dominance, the opportunity to import other items for which there is a local market, and so on. Whatever the medium of exchange, the questions of what terms are reasonable and how they are arrived at must be addressed. The actual acquisition of the desired technology is, of course, only a beginning. Once it is acquired, its acquisition is justified only by successful exploitation. This also requires the commitment of resources, in many instances far larger resources than are available to the developing country, recognizing the breadth of their needs for technology and the limitations on their foreign exchange. The resources involved in this part of the process are customarily expressed in money terms, but in actuality they involve largely human and material resources that may be available to, and controlled by, the developing country's government far more readily than foreign exchange.

If technology is to play its potential key role in development, these four questions must be answered—Where does it come from? Who chooses? How is it acquired? How is to be paid for? But viable answers are not easy to find in the less developed countries. As Herbert Fusfeld, research director of a U.S.–based MNC heavily involved in developing countries, has said in Congressional testimony, "Western science, technology and know-how can be important to developing nations, but not as isolated packages. There must not only be a receiver, but a receiving system with which the transferred package must be compatible. We sometimes talk as if we are throwing a ball to a waiting catcher when we sould be considering the complexities of an organ transplant."

Fusfeld's emphasis on the necessity of a receiving system makes a crucial point. To illustrate its significance, consider the example of agricultural technology and, in particular, the impact of the "Green Revolution." The development of new varieties of maize, wheat, and rice adapted to the growing seasons, soil conditions, water availability, and tilling and harvesting practices of the less developed countries promised a manifold increase in crop yields in those areas. Making the new seed available on a large scale and teaching farmers how to plant it proved not sufficient to release these societies from the shackles of malnutrition. There is much more to the agriculture–food supply system than that. The full benefits of the new seed stocks can be realized only with large-scale applications of fertilizers. Fertilizer plants had to be constructed, requiring further technology, large amounts of capital, and petroleum feed stocks that have become prohibitively expensive to those LDCs that lack indig-

enous sources. Means have to be devised for distributing the fertilizer to the farmers in sufficient quantity and at the right time,
which requires vehicles and roads on a scale not generally available.
Financial arrangements have to be developed to permit the farmers
to buy fertilizer on credit with repayment from the proceeds of the
sale of their increased surpluses. Increased crop yields mean increased storage facilities, protected from the increased number of
rodents that result from greater food production. New transport and
distribution facilities have to be established to bring the new food
surpluses to the cities where they are required. In the cities new
means must be created to make the food available to the poor who
most need it but lack the means to buy it.

The Green Revolution did impact on many LDCs, particularly in
Southeast Asia, but the impacts were in many respects adverse to
the small farmers and the poorest of the urban consumers who were
the intended beneficiaries. For one thing, it was the large (and usually absentee) landowners who possessed the financial resources
and organizational skills to exploit the new technology. The resulting
increased concentration of land holdings, and the introduction of
labor-saving machinery that this made possible, drove many poor
peasants off the land and into urban unemployment. The higher
production of staple grains, and the necessity to export much of the
increase to pay for the imported chemical fertilizers required, had
the effect of tying the LDCs still more closely into the world agricultural economy, where marginal producers are the natural victims of
its ups and downs.

The history of the Green Revolution demonstrates, above all, that
the successful transfer of a new technology, seemingly particularly
appropriate to the priority needs of the less developed countries,
requires and produces alterations in the prevailing socioeconomic
pattern that profoundly impact throughout the society, adversely as
well as beneficially. And these impacts must be confronted by
societies that are deeply resistant to change.

As we shall see, the transfer and utilization of industrial technology for development poses equally complex challenges to both
supplier and recipient nations.

INDUSTRIAL TECHNOLOGY
AND DEVELOPMENT

Almost from the beginnings of conscious attention to the problems
of development and development assistance, it has been widely believed by development planners that industrialization is the road to

development. After all, the obvious feature of a developed country is that it is industrialized. Q.E.D.

Developed countries are not only industrialized, they are generally well-fed and well-educated, have a high degree of social mobility, have low birth rates, have high rates of capital formation, use large amounts of energy, speak a common language, are largely located in the temperate zone, and so on. They are also the generators, possessors, and exploiters of modern technology. Industrialization is certainly not solely responsible for all these features or even a precondition for many of them. Nonetheless, it is there; it is apparent; it is enviable; and, presumably, it is imitable.

At a somewhat more thoughtful level, it has been argued that industrialization is the only way to deal with one of the scourges of underdeveloped nations: unemployment. A UN report in the early 1960s stated: "The reason for emphasizing industrialization is that industrial development would absorb rural underemployed persons." Development planners and economists in both kinds of countries have endorsed this theme. In the long view it is entirely rational. In the case of those countries at the threshold of development, however, the pursuit of this route has not produced the desired benefits and may, in fact, have been counterproductive. As Gunnar Myrdal has pointed out: "For several decades ahead . . . the employment effects of industrialization cannot be expected to be very large. The impact on employment is a function not only of the rate of industrialization but also of the absolute size of industry. For some time the effects may in fact be negative, owing to backlash disemployment of people from traditional industries and crafts that are either competed out or modernized and so made less labor-intensive."[8] Myrdal points out that the intensive Soviet efforts to industrialize their Central Asian republics beginning in the 1920s had this effect and that it persisted until fairly recently, when industrialization finally progressed to a much higher level. Careful studies of the industrialization process have found evidence of the same effects in India and elsewhere.

Industrialization has been notably successful in some developing countries, of course; Israel, Taiwan, Korea, and southeastern Brazil provide dramatic examples. It must be noticed, however, that in each of these cases the circumstances were highly propitious, and each possessed from the start a skilled work force, a well-developed social infrastructure, and considerable experience in international trade. Each relied heavily on imported technology in pursuing the industrialization process.

For the purposes of this book it is important to explore how the international transfer of technology operates in the context of development as a basis for exploring the policy issues involved. Before I do so, it is worthwhile to recall an earlier "development" issue. In the late 1950s and early 1960s a great deal of attention was given to the very rapid rate of economic growth of the United States (and later Japan) in comparison with Western Europe. Even though Europe (with U.S. assistance) had achieved a remarkable recovery from the damage inflicted by World War II, its growth rates, particularly in the advanced technology sectors, remained well below that of the United States. Many politicians and some economists attributed this gap to the demonstrably higher rate of technological innovation that prevailed in the United States at that time; the "technology gap" became a major source of international political debate. In 1967 Edward Denison published the first comprehensive study demonstrating that differences in rate of technological innovation per se could not account for the observed differences in economic performance. He showed that over thirty variables, ranging from health and attitudes toward hours of work ("shifts") to use of capital, were significant determinants of relative economic growth. It would be well for those who seek to attribute the slow growth rates of the LDCs to the antisocial behavior of the industrial sectors in advanced countries to reread the thoughtful analyses of Denison and his followers.[9]

Transfer of Industrial Technology and MNCs

Historically, by far the most significant mechanism for the transfer of industrial technology to the LDCs has been the formation of operating subsidiaries in the LDCs by multinational corporations with the specific purpose of exploiting the opportunities afforded by the local economy—markets and labor and materials resources. In terms of ubiquity and economic impact, the operations of MNCs are far more important than the licensing of technology to unaffiliated firms. For example, cumulative U.S. private investment in developing countries was $28.4 billion in 1974, most of it in subsidiaries of U.S.-based firms, yielding a net investment income of $9.4 billion.[10]

The compelling reasons for the disproportionate importance of MNCs as against the licensing of unaffiliated firms in the international transfer of technology is the undeniable fact that the MNCs transfer technology more effectively and are able, because of their integrated world marketing structures, to take better business advantage of the results of manufacture in the host country than are indigenous firms. (For a more detailed discussion of MNCs and their role in international transfers of technology see Chapter 4.)

For the MNCs the developing countries offer substantial business attractions, particularly low labor costs, and, for those MNCs whose operations involve a large material input, access to raw materials. The frequent absence, in developing countries, of one or more of the other necessary business ingredients—capital, sophisticated technical and managerial skills, and an industrial infrastructure to provide goods and services that support the production operation—is relatively unimportant for the MNCs because of their ability to efficiently organize the international movement of these commodities. The fact that the local market for the goods produced is usually too small to permit taking full advantage of the economies of scale is also relatively less important to a MNC because the MNC is organized to serve a transnational market and because the economies of scale the MNC can exploit in other and larger markets can justify a marginal pricing approach in more limited markets. The combination of these advantages has resulted in a rapid proliferation of MNC subsidiaries in the developing countries.

MNC operations can contribute in significant ways to the progress of the developing host countries. They inject capital and, through the export of the subsidiary's products, foreign exchange.* They create new kinds of employment† and in the course of doing so increase the skill levels of the local labor force through on-the-job experience and more formal training. Their use of local sources of materials, components, and semimanufactured goods provides a broader economic stimulus and frequently results in a diffusion of significant aspects of the parent company's technology to the indigenous economy, particularly through the impact of purchase specifications and standards and acceptance test procedures. Through the training and experience they provide to local professional and supervisory personnel, frequently supplemented by tem-

---

*It is widely alleged that most MNC investment in LDCs is financed from local capital sources and not with new capital from the developed countries. If this were true, it could be asserted that the effect of the creation of a new MNC subsidiary is to drain off capital that might otherwise go to support local entrepreneurs. The validity of this charge is very difficult to test, since data generally are not available. That it is not the usual case would seem to be supported by the fact, which is a matter of public record, that MNCs habitually insist on full equity control of new subsidiaries. MNCs often seek to capitalize locally the earnings of their subsidiaries, because of income tax regulations in their parent countries among other reasons, but this practice would not produce the disbenefit cited. When it is not the creation of an MNC subsidiary that takes place, but the arm's length licensing of technology to a local enterprise, the capital required is often drawn from the local economy, though deferred royalty arrangements, which are sometimes involved, have the effect of lowering the investment capital requirement.

†As Myrdal has pointed out (see note 8), the net effect on local employment may be negative because of the displacement of older, more labor-intensive production.

porary assignment to the parent operation, they contribute to the development of an indigenous entrepreneurial class.[11]

Independent developing country firms import technology through "arm's length" licensing (i.e., that which deals with unaffiliated firms) on a large scale. While most of the technology obtained in this way is directly related to the manufacturing of specific products, other technologies, particularly those related to marketing, make up an important component of the licensing arrangements. Two important categories of such licensed technologies are patents and trademarks. That patents should play an important role is not surprising in light of the fact that most patents registered in the developing countries belong to foreigners, and only a very small proportion of these are actually "worked" in the local economy. The importance of trademarks in licensing arrangements is evidence of the global impact of advertising by the big firms based in the advanced countries; by comparison with the impact of advertising by local firms, the effect is enormous. The importance of trademarks is further reinforced by the tendency of the more affluent classes to prefer products identifiably foreign, as a result of preferences developed in the course of foreign travel or the recognition of better quality, or for less defensible but equally understandable reasons.

The governments of many of the developing countries see the dominant influence of foreign firms, foreign technology, and foreign brand names in their local economies as a threat to their national economic and social progress and aspirations. *Dollar diplomacy* and *neocolonialism* are common characterizations of the situation, reflecting compelling national political perceptions. The United States, whose industrial firms are most often the suppliers of technology to the developing countries, is a major target of these complaints, but the other advanced countries—particularly the United Kingdom, Japan, Germany, and France—also receive intense criticisms.

The rhetoric used by many in the LDCs, however offensive to many politicians and industrialists in the technologically advanced countries, reflects the continued existence of a real problem that must be confronted. Setting aside historical biases and the propensity of many LDCs to acquire symbolic manifestations of technological progress—for example, jet airlines that will never provide the improved transportation systems their countries so badly need—there are many ways in which the global economy operates against the objectives of economic development of the poor countries. Tariff differentials between raw and semifinished materials, for example, work against LDC aspirations for their own mills and refineries, not to mention the creation of a petrochemical industry. Generalized special tariff preferences that lower duties on goods coming from LDCs are only a partial answer, because these arrangements customarily retain the higher duties for processed goods. The LDCs will never achieve their aspirations, and the gaps between rich and poor nations will continue to widen, until means can be found to provide, by import, through indigenous efforts, or, most likely, by a combination of both, the technologies appropriate to the LDCs' factor costs and potential domestic and export markets. Political action is required, by both the LDCs and technologically advanced countries, but it will succeed only if it operates within an economic framework acceptable to all involved.

Developing countries criticize the technology flowing to them from the advanced countries on a commercial basis as inappropriate to their needs; as unfair in the terms and conditions (private and governmental) under which it is supplied; and as having economic and social impacts that are inconsistent with their legitimate aspirations and that cannot be controlled by less than Draconian governmental actions. The evidence in support of these criticisms, as they perceive it, is overwhelming. The fact that the advanced countries (and their industrial enterprises) cite other evidence and judge it differently is, in their view, and as a practical international political problem, largely irrelevant.

Some of the evidence leading to the developing countries' adverse perceptions is anecdotal or draws on incomplete and misinterpreted statistics, but the subject has also been pursued in a more scholarly fashion and with somewhat similar conclusions by competent developing country economists. Generally speaking, payments of royalties and fees for the use of foreign technologies are regarded as excessive, and the bulk of such payments is for technologies that bear little relationship to priority economic needs, as the developing countries perceive them. When linked to investments, total payments for the use of technology often exceed the conventional returns on invested capital. When the licensing of trademarks is involved the arrangements frequently take on the character of a monopoly rent. For example, Mexican officials have found that their firms were paying large royalties abroad for the technology of supermarkets, and one Andean country reports that 30 percent of all its royalties and fees were being paid to foreign pharmaceutical firms. Technology licensing—particularly to unaffiliated firms—frequently takes the form of a package arrangement, so that royalties are paid for portions of the technology that may be already in the public domain or might be acquired more cheaply from other sources. Licensing arrangements often require the licensee to purchase components or intermediary products from the licensor (usually, and sometimes properly, justified as required to maintain adequate quality control); export markets are frequently denied or severely restricted.

These provisions represent to the developing countries, on the one hand, a failure of the parent country to impose on its firms' foreign business dealings the same legal restraints (particularly antitrust laws) as are imposed on domestic operations; and on the other hand, the extraterritorial extension of export restraints that, though required by law in the parent country (e.g., the U.S. Cuban embargo) have no legal basis—and may be in violation of the law—in the recipient nation. They accuse the parent country of arbitrarily applying or failing to apply its own legal principles solely on the basis of the advantages created for its domestic firms in foreign operations. The total impact of the situation, in the developing country view, is to create a technological dependence on the advanced countries inconsistent with their development aspirations. (It is pointed out that annual direct costs for imported technology often exceed twice local R&D expenditures. Frequently the ratio is far higher.)[12]

Legal Controls on Technology Flows

These dissatisfactions have led to the enactment in several developing countries (particularly in Latin America) of legislation specifically designed to control the import of technology. These governments see themselves as responsible both to encourage the acquisition of technology from foreign sources and to exercise a firm control on the terms and conditions for such acquisitions.[13]

Among the first of such legislation was the Foreign Investment Code promulgated in 1970 by the Andean Group (Bolivia, Chile, Colombia, Ecuador, Peru, and subsequently Venezuela).[14] The code requires that member governments should register, authorize, and supervise both foreign investments and the import of technology, and charges members with "evaluating the effective contribution [to national objectives] of the goods incorporating the technology." The specific provisions of the code, which is to be applied retroactively to all contracts with foreign firms, proscribe the inclusion in contracts for technology of many provisions that were previously regarded as customary, including limitations on markets and tie-in purchases, and states that a foreign-based MNC may not receive royalty payments for technology supplied to its subsidiaries in member countries. (Investments in technology are viewed as fully amortized in the parent country domestic market. Continuing R&D investment aimed at the local market, it is felt, should be made in the local subsidiary). The code does not prescribe maximum royalty rates for licensed technology, but leaves that to member governments, who have generally adopted rules limiting royalties to 5 percent of gross sales of the product.

The Andean Code also contemplated major changes in the member governments' patent laws, based on the conclusion that patent rights granted to foreigners provide only disadvantages and no economic benefits to the granting country. An early draft of the code provided that after 1977 the member countries should no longer authorize the registration of any foreign trademarks. These provisions would have involved a form of expropriation, would have contravened existing international treaties and conventions, and would certainly have led to the expulsion of complying member countries from the International Patent Union. So far, they have not been adopted, though they are a reasonable representation of how many developing countries perceive the problems and of the extremes to which they are prepared to go to redress their grievances.

Equally, and in some respects even more, comprehensive controls were enacted by Brazil (1970 and 1971), Argentina (1971), and Mexico (1973), with considerable cross influence.[15] These laws create national authorities with broad powers to screen and regulate contracts involving foreign technology, retroactively as well as in new situations. The antecedants of these laws, and their counterparts in other developing nations, go back to a UN General Assembly resolution adopted in 1961. The General Assembly and other UN bodies—particularly ECOSOC and UNIDO—have pursued the subject area intensely in the years since, publishing guidelines and model contracts for use by the developing countries in the acquisition of foreign technology, and proposals for international *codes of conduct* for MNCs.

Codes of Conduct

The draft "Code of Conduct of the Transfer of Technology" developed by a working group of the Pugwash Conferences on Science and World Affairs in 1974 and widely adopted—with some misgivings by those who felt it didn't go far enough—as a "talking paper" by developing country spokespeople, is exemplary of the political dimensions of the transfer of technology problem. The Pugwash draft code contemplates the development of an international treaty that would bind signatory nations to the legal enforcement of its terms, which are heavily biased toward controls on the suppliers of technology. It would specifically prohibit supplier frms from demanding or enforcing any of the restrictive practices cited above as objectionable to the developing countries, whether through licensing arrangements with unaffiliated firms, through intercorporate arrangements between an MNC parent and its developing country subsidiary, or through recourse to a legal jurisdiction other than that of the developing country. In additon, the Pugwash code would preclude an MNC parent from capitalizing, in the form of equity in a subsidiary, the value of the technology supplied or its share of profits earned. Further, the code would contravene, or require alteration of, those provisions of the Paris Convention on Intellectual Property providing that patentees may exert, as a right deriving from their patent, control on import and use of the patented item from another country. It must be acknowledged that many of the other restrictive practices by technology suppliers that would be prohibited by the Pugwash code are, in the United States, prohibited by antitrust legislation insofar as they might affect domestic competition or the foreign trade of this country.

The Pugwash code is largely silent on the question of responsibilities of recipient governments. Nothing is said, for example, about security of foreign investment, repatriation of earnings, or protection of intellectual property (patents, copyrights, and trademarks). This lack of reciprocity accounts for a large part of the opposition to the Pugwash code by advanced country firms. Certain of the specific provisions are unacceptable to them as written, and the notion of a legally binding code applicable to every international industrial technology transfer is widely—and in all likelihood, correctly—regarded as ill-informed at best.

Private sector interests have responded by publishing *guidelines* intended as alternatives to legally binding *codes* and emphasizing reciprocity, that is, the rights of technology suppliers and the responsibilities of recipient governments as well as firms. The Pacific Basin Economic Council (composed of senior business executives from Australia, Canada, Japan, New Zealand, and the United States) and the International Chamber of Commerce have played leading roles in this effort.[16]

Pressures for adoption of a binding code of conduct are building in various international forums, particularly in the various UN organizations dominated by development concerns. After some years of refusing even to discuss these matters in such organizations, in 1975 the advanced countries recognized the political necessity of a change in approach and began consultations among themselves on guidelines for voluntary compliance by MNCs, dealing with most of the issues raised by the LDCs but adding provisions regarding the responsibilities of host governments. The latter provisions concentrate on the questions of national treatment for foreign investors and on the difficult issue of international arbitration of disputes.

The issue of codes of conduct for the international transfer of industrial technology is by no means resolved. There is great pressure in UN organizations and elsewhere for the development of legally binding principles. The increasing disparities among national legislative treatments of these matters does demonstrate a need for international rationalization, but the differences of perspective between technology-supplier and technology-receiver countries—exacerbated by the ideological proclivities of the secretariats of the UN organizations involved—make a productive dialogue on these issues particularly difficult.

TECHNOLOGY ASSISTANCE STRATEGIES

There can be no question that the technologically advanced countries have a special ability to contribute to the progress of development. Neither can it be argued that such a policy is not in the political interest of the advanced nations. Not only do the advanced nations have a major stake in international political stability and in the service of humanitarian goals, but also, on a more pragmatic level, the advanced country economies are increasingly dependent on the availability of raw materials (including fuels) that are heavily concentrated in the less developed nations.

The historic, economic, cultural, and political gulfs that separate the advanced industrial countries (read the United States) from the developing countries (read one's own preference) are profound. For the majority of the developing countries, these gaps seem to be widening rather than closing. Furthermore, no one in either kind of country seems to have a sure and credible grasp of the socioeconomic dynamics that operate to move some nations—Mexico, Taiwan, Korea, Israel, for example—out of the underdeveloped category with impressive momentum, while apparently consigning the remainder to an increasingly underprivileged and dependent status. In light of this confusion, assigning priorities to technical assistance possibilities is a chancey, perhaps foolhardy, exercise. At the same time, it appears incontrovertible that the advanced countries must face a responsibility in this respect that is unavoidable and increasingly urgent.

For the least developed, and perhaps for all of the less developed nations, relief from the straitjacket of the nutrition-health-population dilemma is the most basic problem, even though the impacts, political as well as substantive, of progress in this area will be slow to be realized. (Demographic analysis demonstrates an intrinsic time delay between a decrease in birth rate and a resulting reduction in population growth rate of approximately one generation.)

Of the subelements of this cycle, health has made the greatest progress, through the combined (if not optimally coordinated) efforts of the World Health Organization, the programs of AID in the United States, and its counterparts in other donor nations, and the major efforts of the foundations, universities, and other organizations in the private sector.

Food and nutrition have received major attention but have proven more resistant to progress, probably because progress in these areas involves intervention at more points in the socioeconomic system of the LDCs than does health care, an area more highly institutionalized in the developing, as in the advanced, countries.

The population growth problem has had major attention in the national priorities of the advanced countries as well as in international organizations, particularly the UN. In contrast to the other elements of the cycle, population issues take on social, religious, and political overtones of major significance. The failure of the UN World Population Conference in 1975 to achieve unanimity even on the principle of population planning reflects just these obstacles.

The industrial sector poses special challenges for technology assistance. The implications of differences in cultures and in socioeconomic structures for policy development are, at best, imperfectly understood by policy-making officials in both developing and advanced countries.

Too much attention, in all likelihood, has been given to the "science" dimension of technical assistance, a situation that developed naturally from the fact that it was largely the academic scientific community of the advanced countries that first seized the challenge of development. The result has too often been a focus on support for graduate education and the creation of indigenous research institutions that have no established relationship with the productive sectors of developing societies. As Herbert Fusfeld has said in commenting on the relationship of science to the problems of development:

It is, of course, true that in any specific instance a new scientific [discovery] can lead to a major development which can result in a new business or a new industry. But in the broad sense, basic research *follows* applied research, and research and development *follow* industry. That is, once an industrial base is established, money and manpower can be devoted to R&D because the system for using the results is in place. Once a major development is well underway, there is increased justification and pressure for basic research and a sharper definition of the particular areas of basic research where new knowledge would be most helpful. The appreciation of this overall system has often been lacking in discussions of technology transfer, leading to disappointment and wasted effort at best, and possibly to charges of "window dressing" and "bad faith."[17]

Technology Receiving Systems: The KIST Approach

The ability to receive successfully modern technology is achievable, as demonstrated in a number of instances. One of the most frequently cited successes is KIST, initiated in 1966 by the joint efforts of the Korean Ministry of Science and Technology and the U.S. National Academy of Sciences, with financial support by AID. One of KIST's strategies, in particular, would seem to merit careful consideration in development planning in other countries. KIST typically initiates the process of developing requirements for technology acquisition from abroad by conducting an in-depth survey of a particular sector of the economy recognized as important to longer term national development goals, for instance, the foundry sector. The survey is undertaken by an ad hoc team of market economists, technical specialists, and managers experienced in the particular sector. (Short-term consulting assistance from an industrially advanced country is used to fill out any gaps in locally available competence.) All national firms active in the sector are visited and analyzed. The purposes of the survey, which starts from an agreed estimate of the total demand for sectoral output five to ten years ahead, are several:

- To establish accurately the state of the art of the technology currently employed.
- To establish the increase in sectoral productivity necessary to meet the estimated future market demand starting from the present industrial base.
- To establish the improvement in quality and uniformity of the product necessary to meet the anticipated demands, and the price

increase per unit of production that could be justified by such improvements.

- To establish the availability of adequate supplies of necessary raw materials and the steps necessary to meet any shortfall.
- To determine the necessary training or reeducation of personnel at all levels required to achieve the desired production growth.
- To quantify the requirement for additional capital investment necessary to the expansion of production.

Only after this analysis has been completed are the questions of the necessity for imported technology, the exact technology required, the responsibility for handling the acquisition, and the specific training required for local personnel identified.

The KIST approach has a number of important characteristics:

- It starts from specific priorities and objectives established by the competent government authorities, in consultation with industry.
- It engages the host government, the recipient firms, the indigenous analytical and technical competence, and—where appropriate—expert assistance from potential technology supplier governments in an analytical effort to which each becomes committed before implementation plans (whether for additional capital investment, training, or technology acquisition) are finalized.
- It provides built-in means for monitoring and measuring the success of the total undertaking.

It should be noted that in the Korean approach, the decision to move forward in the acquisition of specific foreign technology, with all of the necessary corollary commitments, is often accompanied by the creation of a supporting technology institute, frequently associated with a university, specifically charged with responsibilities for the success of the plan ultimately agreed on. The initial leadership of such specialist institutes is often drawn from the membership of the ad hoc study team. Korea also has adopted the practice of recruiting Korean nationals living abroad who have received relevant advanced training to provide the technical leadership of the study team and the resulting institute. These arrangements are customarily on a term basis, but the Korean experience has been that many individuals recruited in this way remain permanently—an example of successful reversal of the "brain drain."

Joseph Mintzes has examined the overall economic impacts on the

Table 6.1

Average Annual Growth for Selected Technological Development Indicators, 1967–1973

	Colombia	Mexico	Korea	Japan
GNP	6.4%	6.7%	11.4%	10.4%
GNP per capita	3.0	3.3	9.3	9.2
Manufacturing index	7.7	7.7	23.0	12.4
Per capita electric power consumption	6.0	7.1	16.2	9.0
Payments to U.S. and Japanese firms for licensed technology*	9.3	8.6	37.9	21.6

*Payments to Japan are negligible except for Korea's, which are larger than those it made to the United States. Korea also obtains significant amounts of technology from other nations, particularly Germany.

SOURCE: Joseph Mintzes, *Licensing R&D and Technology Development in Selected Developing Countries*. Washington, D.C.: Office of Science and Technology, Agency for International Development, August 1974 (unpublished report).

Korean strategy (which involves other elements beyond the KIST operations) in comparison with the results achieved under different foreign technology strategies in Mexico, Colombia, and Japan.[18] (The last named is hardly a developing country. As a country relying heavily on imported technology and enjoying a remarkable rate of economic growth, however, it provides an interesting datum point.) Table 6.1 summarizes Mintzes' data comparing selected technological development indicators for these countries for the period 1967–1973. The data given in the table are incomplete for a variety of reasons; the principal effect is to understate payments for technology.

It is clear from these data that a high level of technology importing can be associated with extraordinarily rapid growth in overall and per capita GNP. It is also evident that these growth rates are primarily associated with rapid industrialization. It is not possible, of course, to assert—on the basis of these data, in any event—that the growth was due to the import of technology. Trade, investment, education, natural resource endowments, and various economic and social factors also have important, though not quantifiable, bearing on technological progress.

Mintzes' comparative analysis also shows that the cost of the imported technology involved in the Korean success need not be a barrier to other LDCs. Of the countries examined Korea's payments for imported technology, as a proportion of export earnings, were the smallest, about $1/15$ that of Mexico, $1/8$ that of Japan, and $1/3$ that of Columbia. Neither was Korea's total investment in R&D high by familiar standards. In 1971, for example, Korea spent 0.56 percent of GNP on R&D, as compared with 1.4 percent by Japan and 2.8 percent by the U.S. Korea spent eight times as much on indigenous R&D as on imported technology. In contrast, Mexico spent significantly more on imported technology than on indigenous R&D, and Colombia spent nine times as much on imported technology than in its own R&D laboratories. The significance of these comparisons is not easy to particularize, but it seems reasonable to hypothesize that Korea's national planning in this regard was more careful, and accordingly much more successful, than Colombia's or Mexico's.

Technology Transfer to the Resource-Rich LDCs

As mentioned earlier, certain countries, especially the petroleum-exporting nations of the Middle East, are both extraordinarily rich (on a per capita basis) and underdeveloped in almost every other sense. Though possessed of large numbers of jet aircraft and high-powered automobiles, they are typically characterized by extremes of social stratification with only a tiny minority of their population educated and provided with adequate nutrition and the rudiments of health care. Incongruously, although their populations are generally small, unemployment is high. This is often a reflection of deeply rooted cultural and religious traditions that reserve particular kinds of occupations to limited classes of people. Even the limited accouterments of technology already in place often require the massive import of foreign labor to operate and maintain it.

The political leaders of these countries, usually educated in Europe or the United States, see technology as the key to their national development and an answer to ultimate depletion of their natural resources. Foreign exchange to acquire it is no problem, and the advanced countries, eager to cover the skyrocketing costs of essential imported petroleum, are more than willing to supply whatever technology is desired. However, the lack of an adequate receiving system is as great an obstacle in these countries as in the other LDCs. (Only the capacity to absorb huge quantities of modern armaments seems to be unlimited.) The United States, like the other advanced countries, has rushed to help these nations. The difference between the ability to buy and the ability to use technology effectively is profound, however, and the successful modernization of these countries, in other than a most superficial way, will take many years at best.

Suppose the effort is successful; will that build a more stable world? Will the creation of a fully integrated petrochemical industry in the Middle Eastern countries make political, economic, and military relationships in the region or between the oil producers and the advanced nations more contentious or less? Will the resource-poor LDCs benefit, or will they become even more dependent on concessional aid to arrest the decay and avoid eventual collapse of their societies? The answers to these questions are by no means predictable. Failure to find acceptable answers will be disastrous.

The U.S. Government and Technology Assistance

In absolute terms, the United States has been by far the largest donor of governmental-financed technology assistance to the developing countries, although measured in relationship to GNP, U.S. contributions rank well below those of Sweden, the Netherlands, France, Norway, Australia, Denmark, Canada, Belgium, and the United Kingdom.[19] In 1974 U.S. official bilateral and multilateral development assistance amounted to $3.4 billion. The United States is far and away the largest supplier of industrial technology through commercial licensing and foreign investment. In spite of (or conceivably because of) this dominant role, U.S. efforts in technology assistance are frequently criticized as inadequate, inappropriate, or counterproductive from all sides (including several important domestic constituencies).

AID operates under strict Congressionally mandated constraints in the conduct of its assistance programs. The Foreign Assistance Act of 1976 not only limits the total number of countries with whom AID is authorized to develop assistance programs but excludes some countries by name. AID is directed to concentrate on programs benefiting the poor in each recipient country: food and agriculture, health and nutrition, and rural development. The International Security Assistance and Arms Export Control Act of 1976 invokes a "human rights" condition on both military and economic assistance, with certain escape clauses. Specifically, the law makes ineligible for assistance those countries that "grossly and consistently violate the integrity of individuals" as defined by the UN Universal Declaration of Human Rights, requiring a regular report from the Department of State on the status of human rights in the eighty-two countries that might receive some form of assistance. Release of the first report in 1977 provoked Argentina, Brazil, Uruguay, Guatemala, and El Salvador to publicly reject planned U.S. military assistance; the amounts budgeted were, in any event, quite small.

As pointed out earlier, the U.S. government is severely constrained in its choice of strategies for development assistance by the overriding reality that both the sources of the needed technology and the know-how to apply it successfully to real problems lie largely in the private sector. Elaborate schemes for industrial development institutes, technical information centers, and the like can only nibble at the edges of this reality and run the substantial political risk that, however lavishly supported with public funds, they may in the end only exacerbate the frustrations of foreign and domestic politicians alike.

Public Sector Technologies in Development

There is a broad spectrum of technologies important to the progress of development that lie wholly within the purview of governments in both the advanced and developing countries. These are the technologies associated with public services. A comprehensive listing would fill pages, but a few examples will illustrate what is meant:

- Air traffic control
- Building construction standards
- Emergency health care delivery
- Fire prevention and fire fighting
- Forestry management
- Highway planning and engineering
- Meat and poultry inspection
- Water quality maintenance
- Weather observation and forecasting

Such public service technologies exist in an operating structure within each advanced country government. The structure in each case provides for planning; development of standards for compliance with legal or regulatory requirements; procedures for conducting the necessary field operations to insure compliance; training of specialist personnel at all levels; and, of course, the necessary management and supervisory capabilities.

From the standpoint of programs for government-to-government technical assistance for development, these public service technologies offer several advantages: They relate to essential aspects of the development of a governmental infrastructure. They do not involve the complexities of proprietary industrial technologies. They are essentially soft technologies, represented by procedures and know-how that exist in the relevant government departments and agencies. Since the technology exists and is regularly practiced in these agencies, a built-in capability for providing consultative services and appropriate training to developing country nationals is already at hand. Finally, and of no small importance, the transfer of these technologies does not require the creation of new institutional and administrative structures and is, therefore, inexpensive.

Donor governments have a central role in the planning and organization of training at many levels as a component of development assistance. One of the most important aspects is higher education in the full range of relevant technical and managerial fields.[20] Each of the donor countries has established programs in this area. These massive programs have been a vital contribution to the development process, but they are nonetheless the subject of considerable controversy.

A principal complaint from the developing countries is that the programs stimulate a "brain drain." Students who have become used to living in the advanced countries and have developed there professional skills for which they can find no suitable outlet in their home countries are, understandably, reluctant to return. The result is a defeat of both donor and recipient countries' intentions. The problem has its origins in two facts: The curricula available in most advanced country colleges and universities are not adapted to the real needs of the developing countries, and the entire educational environment to which these students are exposed reflects cultural attitudes and social assumptions that are profoundly different from those in their home countries. The students who come from the developing countries are carefully selected for their educational potential—as they should be—and frequently turn out to be among the best performers in their classroom programs. The sense of achievement this creates is, of course, basic to any student's educational progress. Unfortunately, achievements in the higher educational environment of the advanced countries are no guarantee of the opportunity for similar or comparable achievements at home. An alternative approach that offers greater promise of achieving the desired contribution to development is for the donor countries to organize and provide the necessary human and financial resources to create the desired technical education in developing country institutions. With this approach it is the professor who must adapt to a strange environment, rather than the students. More students can be trained, since direct costs are lower, and the in situ approach also contributes an important side benefit in the stimulus it provides to the development of the indigenous universities. The principal difficulty of this approach is the problem of finding suitably qualified instructors who are willing to devote a period of two or three years (one year is too short to be wholly effective) to such a foreign assignment.

The need and urgency of development in the two-thirds of the world's population that is poorly fed, largely illiterate, underemployed, frustrated, and grows in numbers at an alarming rate is undeniable. The advanced countries have a major responsibility to assist in the process, not only from humanitarian motivations but because of their vital self-interests in assured sources of needed fuels and raw materials and the export markets that provide the earnings to pay for these imports. World political stability is a concern to all.

Technology has an important place in the development process, but the technology transfer mechanisms that link the advanced nations apparently break down when applied to transfer to the LDCs. Differences in resource availability, cultural affinities, social goals, and, above all, the absence of a receiving system for modern technology in the LDCs call for new approaches; but the nature of successful approaches remains elusive. In an interdependent world we have no option but to press on with the search for solutions.

Notes

1. Katz, S. Stanley. The Developing World and U.S. Trade. *The International Essays for Business Decision Makers, 1976.* Dallas: Southern Methodist University, 1976.

2. Pearson, Lester B., chairman. *Partners in Development: Report of the Commission on International Development.* New York: Praeger, 1969, p. 358.

3. McNamara, Robert S. Address to the Board of Governors: September 1, 1975. Washington, D.C.: World Bank.

4. UN Economic and Social Council. Document E/4178, 41st Session, 1971.

5. For alternative definitions, compare: Emanuel deKadt and Gavin Williams (eds.), *Sociology and Development.* London: Tavistock, 1974; also Irma Adelman and Cynthia T. Morris, *Economic Growth and Social Equity in Developing Countries.* Stanford, Calif.: Stanford University Press, 1973. For a thoughtful synthesis of the findings of these and several related studies see *The Economist,* September 7, 1974, 111ff.

6. Of the voluminous material on appropriate technologies for development, perhaps the one that best illuminates the policy issues and the difficulties encountered in resolving them is *Choice and Adaptation of Technology in Developing Countries.* Paris: Development Centre, Organisation for Economic Co-operation and Development, 1974. For a useful discussion of the practical problems involved, focusing on the Latin American experience, see Simon Teitel, Notes on the Transfer and Adaptation of Technology in Latin America with Special Reference to Industrial Development in the 50s and 60s. *Colloques Internationaux C.N.R.S.*, No. 538. Paris: Centre National de la Recherche Scientifique, 1970.

7. Unpublished data from the U.S. Agency for International Development.

8. Myrdal, Gunnar. The Transfer of Technology to Underdeveloped Countries. *Scientific American,* 1974, **231,** 172ff.

9. Denison, Edward F., with Poullier, Jean-Pierre. *Why Growth Rates Differ: Postwar Experience in Nine Western Countries.* Washington, D.C.: The Brookings Institution, 1967. See also Keith Pavitt and Salomon Wald, *The Conditions for Success in Technological Innovation.* Paris: Organisation for Economic Co-operation and Development, 1971; and Jean-Pierre Poullier, The Myth and Challenge of the Technological Gap, in the Atlantic Institute, *The Technology Gap: U.S. and Europe.* New York: Praeger, 1970.

10. *International Economic Report of the President.* Washington, D.C.: Council on International Economic Policy, 1976, pp. 66, 158.

11. For valuable case studies of the actual experience of MNCs in transferring technology to LDCs, see Jack N. Behrman and Harvey W. Wallendar, *Transfers of Manufacturing Technology Within Multinational Enterprises.* Cambridge, Mass.: Ballinger, 1975.

12. *Major Issues Arising From the Transfer of Technology to Developing Countries.* UN Conference on Trade and Development. Document TD/B/AC.11/10/ Rev 1, 1974.

13. Driscoll, Robert E., and Wallendar, Harvey W., eds. *Technology Transfer and Development: An Historical and Geographic Perspective.* New York: Fund for Multinational Management Education and the Council of the Americas, 1974. For a discussion of the development of *U.S.* policies for MNC paticipation in the LDCs see Mira Wilkins, *The Maturing of Multinational Enterprise: American Business Abroad from 1914 to 1970.* Cambridge, Mass.: Harvard University Press, 1977, pp. 327ff.

14. Behrman, Jack N. *Decision Criteria for Foreign Direct Investment in Latin America.* New York: Council of the Americas, 1974.

15. Behrman, *Decision Criteria.*

16. Perlmutter, Howard V. *The Perplexing Routes to Legitimacy: Codes of Conduct for MNEs Regarding Technology Transfer and Development.* Philadelphia: The Wharton School Multinational Enterprise Unit, University of Pennsylvania, 1976. See also Susan S. Holland (ed.), *Codes of Conduct for the Transfer of Technology: A Critique.* New York: Council of the Americas and Fund for Multinational Management Education, 1976.

17. Fusfeld, Herbert. Unpublished memorandum, 1976.

18. Mintzes, Joseph. Licensing R&D and Technology Development in Selected Developing Countries (unpublished report). Washington, D.C.: Office of Science and Technology, Agency for International Development, August 1974.

19. Hansen, Roger D., ed. *The U.S. and World Development: Agenda for Action—1976.* New York: Praeger (published for the Overseas Development Council), 1976, p. 204.

20. Board on Science and Technology for International Development. *The Role of U.S. Engineering Schools in Development Assistance.* Washington, D.C.: National Research Council, 1976.

7

INTERNATIONAL POLITICS, ENERGY, AND CRITICAL MATERIALS

In recent years it has become obvious that the consumption of non-renewable material resources is rising at a faster rate than world population and that the uneven global patterns of supply and consumption are a driving force of international politics and a potential source of international confrontation. Rates of material consumption rise with population growth, of course, but more than population growth is involved. High technology–based lifestyles require raw materials and energy disproportionate to the number of people involved. The United States and Western Europe, with one-eighth of the global population, consume roughly half of global fuel and mineral production. Even for food and water, the most basic materials, the meat-based diets and lavish residential and industrial water usage typical of the advanced countries lead to per capita consumption far larger than that in impoverished countries.

Maldistribution of food supply is basically an economic problem, which is not to say that it is an easy problem. Global production is adequate to feed the whole world; the difficulty is that those who need more food—the poor everywhere—do not have the money to buy it. Wider diffusion, especially to the LDCs, of modern production, processing, storage, and distribution technologies is a necessary, but not a sufficient, condition for solving the problem.[1]

I will focus in this chapter on nonrenewable (mineral) resources and fossil fuels. The international political problems in this area are complex and difficult. They arise from the well-known fact that economically exploitable reserves of a large number of materials critical to technology-based economies are not distributed globally in the same patterns as they are consumed. Only the United States and the U.S.S.R., of the populous nations, possess natural resources generally adequate to their needs. For the rest of the world, there is a great discrepancy between production and consumption patterns; for many critical materials and for petroleum production, sources are largely located in the LDCs.

The role of technology in these matters, while not as important in most instances as political factors, is nonetheless important, primarily because it is the commitment to certain kinds of technology (and the useful and relatively inexpensive products derived from them) that creates the market for "critical" materials and fuels. With sufficient incentives, technology can also provide means for conserving scarce materials or substituting more abundant ones. Technology is vital to the discovery and extraction of mineral resources and fuels. Most important, perhaps, progress in technology offers the long-term promise of virtual independence from fossil fuels as energy sources.

The global materials system, with its exceedingly complex technological, economic, environmental, and political ramifications, raises a host of public policy issues that are remarkably resistant to the leverage of particular policy instruments. (The "success" of the OPEC embargo of 1973–1974 was, more than anything else, the result of skillful timing of an unexpected policy move. In the end, the global economy proved more insensitive—*inelastic*, in economic terms—to oil prices than the conventional wisdom of the 1960s could have accepted.) In particular, the fact that high-technology products employ a much smaller materials input in relation to other costs than do low-technology products—that is, the markets for high-technology products are relatively insensitive to the costs of materials and energy inputs—limits the utility of technological strategies in the international political arena. Another limitation results from the capital-intensive and obsolescence-prone nature of many high-technology products and processes. In light of these factors, the discussion of minerals and oil that follow offer little support for the notion that greater government emphasis on new technologies will relieve the traumas of global interdependence.

It is true, of course, that proven reserves of petroleum and of mineral ores exploitable at what are now conceived as acceptable costs are limited, and once consumed, fossil fuels and a high proportion of essential metals are forever lost through irreversible chemical change or dissipation. This basic problem, accepted as real by nearly every analyst, is seen in quite different terms by those approaching it from different perspectives.[2]

On the one hand, there are those who see the problem in terms of "limits to growth" that promise catastrophic consequences if the world does not adopt new ways. On the other hand, most traditional economists see "grounds for optimism (albeit qualified) that technology will solve problems of exploration, extraction, substitution, and environmental impact."[3] The antithesis of the two views reflects a basic difference in time horizons; the "limits" group calibrate their findings in centuries, or perhaps millenia; the traditional economists think in terms of years or decades.[4] Without engaging in this very important debate, we will look somewhat more closely at selected issues in the critical fuels and minerals area: their relationships to national interests and global politics and the promise, if any, that technology offers for moderating, if not alleviating, them.

MINERAL RESOURCES

Availability

The known chemical composition of the accessible portions of the earth's crust and of the oceans suggests almost unlimited resources of minerals. Unfortunately, the suggestion is not a helpful one for several reasons. The first is the vital distinction between *resources* (in the sense just used) and *reserves*—known locations of ores, economically exploitable with present technology, and in amounts that are forecastable with reasonable confidence. The relationships between the two measures and the external variables involved are elegantly illustrated in a diagram developed by Vincent McKelvey, a former director of the U.S. Geological Survey (Figure 7.1). Beyond the basic relationships among mineral reserves, available technology, and economic costs illustrated in the figure, other important considerations intrude. Lower grade ores inevitably require more energy input to extract the desired minerals. (The largest energy demand is simply in crushing the necessary amounts of rock, but the various techniques for separating the base metal from its mineral form require considerable energy outlays also.) Frequently vast quantities of water are involved in the refining processes, and major mineral deposits have a remarkable propensity for turning up where water is

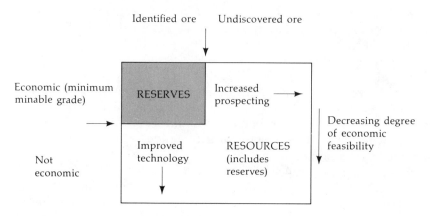

Figure 7.1
The Relationship Between Mineral Resources and Reserves
(SOURCE: *U.S. Geological Survey*).

scarce. The huge amounts of useless rubble left in mine tailings are, at a minimum, unsightly, and they often pollute the groundwater in ways dangerous to plant and animal life.

There are political considerations as well. The main reserves of critical minerals are seldom located in the advanced industrial countries; they are often found in countries that, for a variety of reasons, are politically unstable and not as dependable a source of supply as the advanced governments would choose for a well-ordered world. The maps in Figure 7.2 show the picture. The current and foreseeable dependence of most of the technologically advanced countries on foreign sources of uncertain reliability for many minerals critical to their industrial production (and, not incidentally, their defense systems) is very real. 1974 figures for U.S. mineral dependence on imports from LDCs and communist countries, taken together, are given in Table 7.1. The United States is generally rich in minerals compared to Western Europe and Japan. Of the basic industrial minerals, the European Community and Japan import essentially all of their requirements except for modest indigenous mining of lead and zinc and, in the case of the EC, aluminum and iron.

Political Problems and Technological "Fixes"

The political problems associated with mineral import dependence include assurance of supply (including the possibility of cartel actions and embargoes), stability in prices, and the threat of expropria-

Table 7.1
Mineral Imports from LDCs and Communist Countries

Minerals	Percentage of U.S. Consumption
Columbium	97%
Tin	79
Aluminum	63
Manganese	55
Cobalt	50
Chromium	46
Tungsten	39
Platinum	28

SOURCE: *International Economic Report of the President*, 1976, p. 96

tion of the massive investments the advanced countries have made in foreign mines. It is beyond the scope of this book to discuss these issues,[5] except to note that the total world trade in ores and minerals is less than half that in agricultural raw materials, about one-seventh that in food, less than one-fourth that in fuels, and hardly one-twenty-fifth that in manufactured goods (1974 figures).[6] There can be no doubt, however, that over time absolute shortages or spiraling prices of certain critical materials—copper, tin, and lead, for example—will pose major adjustment difficulties for certain industrial sectors.

Technology can provide relief, through improvements in recovery from lower grade ores or from recycling of used metals, by devising substitute materials, by reducing the dissipation of critical materials through nonessential uses that diffuse the material so widely that recovery and reuse is impossible (40 percent of all zinc production goes to galvanizing, for example), or by extending product life. None of these technological fixes are without complications, however. Consider design for longer product life as an illustration. The modern automobile, with an average life of about five years, is a prime example of profligate use of materials.[7] A substantial increase in service life would be technically straightforward, though consumer acceptability may not be. The economic impact on GNP and employment would be very substantial: In the United States automobile manufacturing accounts for roughly 4.2 percent of manufacturing employment and 5.5 percent of GNP. Cutting this production in half by doubling highway life, however received by owner–drivers, clearly would pose major adjustment problems for the economy. The proper words, however, are not *would pose* but *will pose*; the change is inevitable, along with changes in many equally visible aspects of our materials economy. The question is when.

132

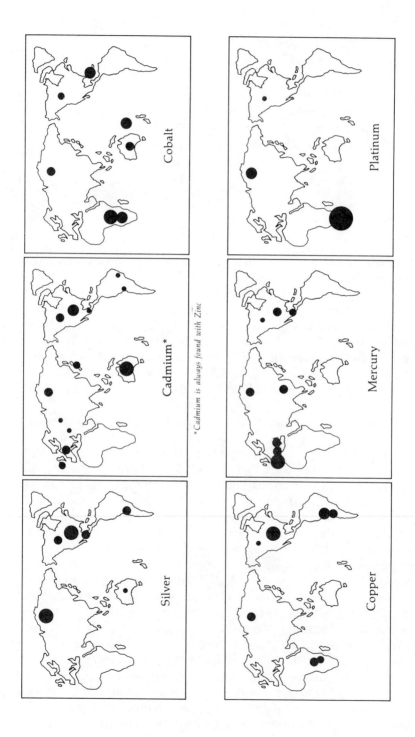

*Cadmium is always found with Zinc

133

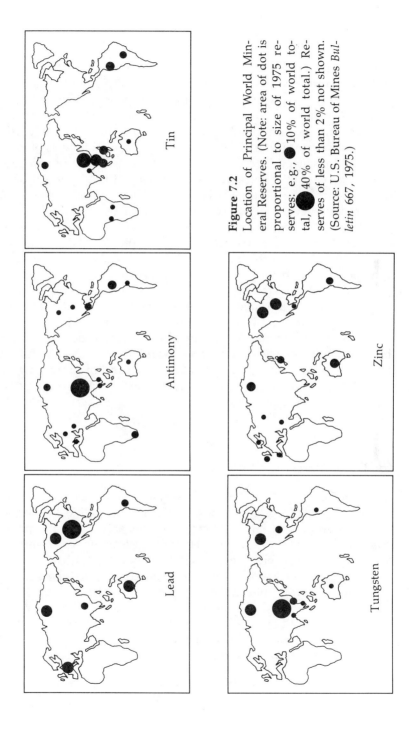

Figure 7.2
Location of Principal World Mineral Reserves. (Note: area of dot is proportional to size of 1975 reserves; e.g., ● 10% of world total, ⬤ 40% of world total.) Reserves of less than 2% not shown. (Source: U.S. Bureau of Mines *Bulletin* 667, 1975.)

Tin

Antimony

Lead

Zinc

Tungsten

OIL

Between early October 1973 and January 1974 the posted prices of Middle Eastern crude oil rose from \$3.01 to \$11.65 per barrel. In that period also the Arab suppliers invoked selective quotas and embargoes against those nations supporting Israel in the Mid East conflict. Thus did the thirteen members of the Organization of Petroleum Exporting Countries (OPEC)* demonstrate the global politics of natural resource diplomacy. The impacts were dramatic. In economic terms, within one year oil exports rose from 5 percent to 13 percent of total world exports, the oil import bill of the United States rose \$15 billion, and higher oil prices cost the nonoil LDCs \$10 billion, more than their 1974 receipts of concessional aid.[8] Foreign ministers in Western Europe and Japan toured Arab capitals to barter for preferential treatment, offering as inducements access to advanced technology and (from the Europeans) armaments. Long lines appeared at U.S. gas stations, and New England was threatened with a chilly winter. The remarkable price inelasticity of oil was quickly demonstrated, but not before the resonating inflationary impact of a 387 percent price increase had tipped the Western democracies into the worst inflationary slough since World War II.[9] Meanwhile, the threat of further embargoes (not yet realized) and of continuing price escalation (held in check loosely only by the Saudis, a small population of strict Moslems who have difficulty spending the money) remained.

The World Energy Conference

It was Secretary of State Henry Kissinger who seized the opportunity of the crisis to press for new levels of joint political action with Western Europe and Japan. Henry Nau has articulated the paradox involved in the U.S. initiative: "Though least dependent of all Western countries on foreign energy supplies and embarked upon a domestic energy program—Project Independence—to eliminate this dependence altogether in 10–15 years, the United States has stressed more widely and more frequently than any other Western country the condition of international interdependence and the requirement for international cooperation in the field of energy."[10] After considering and rejecting several varyingly plausible explana-

---

*Iran, Iraq, Kuwait, Qatar, Saudi Arabia, and the United Arab Emirates (the OAPEC group); Algeria, Gabon, Libya, and Nigeria; Ecuador, Venezuela, and Indonesia.

tions of this attitude, including particularly the fear that other primary resource-producing groups, inspired by the OPEC example, might invoke cartel powers similarly threatening, Nau concludes that Kissinger (presumably with the support of President Nixon) sought what were primarily political–diplomatic gains for which these officials were "willing to pay a substantial technological and economic price." Clearly, both areas of inducement played conspicuous roles in the strategy that evolved. The long-run costs of both were tempered, however, by U.S. leadership in the technological area and the relative insulation of the U.S. economy from the play of the international oil market. The goals were the familiar ones: West European acceptance of the U.S. definition of an acceptable Arab–Israeli settlement, detente between the superpowers, and recognition of U.S. political-economic-security interests in Europe.*

Kissinger convened the Washington (later transmuted to "the World") Energy Conference in February 1974. In attendance were representatives of the major OECD countries. Until the eve of the conference, Kissinger was at odds on strategy with William E. Simon, then Deputy Secretary of the Treasury and for two months head of the Federal Energy Office, and with Dixy Lee Ray, then chairman of the Atomic Energy Commission and principal author of Project Independence.[11] Simon and Ray believed that U.S. natural and technological resources were equal to the Arab challenge, and found difficulty in accepting Kissinger's view that bigger stakes were involved. Kissinger prevailed, and the United States entered the conference with a strategy of offering U.S. technology as an inducement for a commitment by the other OECD members to political solidarity in the face of the OPEC challenge. Only France and Belgium resisted. (The latter came around.) What emerged, after months of intensive negotiation, was a duality: the International Energy Program (IEP) and the International Energy Agency (IEA), organized in November 1974 under the authority of, but not embracing all of the membership of, the OECD.

The IEP/IEA

The principal details are worth reciting here, because the IEP/IEA provides a classic example of both the potentials and problems of international cooperation and of the promise of technological coop-

---

*It is unfair to link Professor Nau with this definition of U.S. goals. His paper permits this interpretation, but it is my particular listing given here.

eration in return for political collaboration. The IEP, in addition to other measures less significant in this context, pledged the 12 signatories* to:

- Common action to limit individual and collective vulnerability to interruptions in the supply of imported petrolem through integrated contingency arrangements.
- A long-term program to reduce dependence on imported oil through conservation, stimulation of capital investment, development of additional or alternative sources of supply, energy-related research and development, and cooperative measures for uranium enrichment.

The contingency program is important in this context because it is the political quid pro quo for which technological cooperation was the primary inducement. The contingency program was demanding, requiring of each signatory a commitment to:

- Emergency self-sufficiency (i.e., the ability to survive without oil imports for a fixed period of time—initially 60 days) by reliance on emergency stocks, standby production facilities, and alternate fuels.
- Emergency demand restraint (i.e., agreement to reduce consumption during an emergency by a common percentage, this action to be automatically triggered by any artificially provoked shortfall to group imports).
- Emergency sharing, in event of a general supply or *a selective embargo against any member or group of members* (emphasis added).

These measures obviously entail both considerable economic commitment and the risk of forceful domestic political opposition to the governments involved if they should be implemented. Clearly, the energy crisis—and the possibility of its resumption—were seen as major threats to national well-being by each of the signatories. Nonetheless, the measures agreed on were far-reaching to a degree unprecedented in peacetime. How could the United States, to whom the economic and political cost would be the least relative to its resource endowments and economic strength, persuade the Euro-

*Belgium, Canada, Denmark, Germany, Ireland, Italy, Japan, Luxembourg, the Netherlands, Norway, United Kingdom, and the United States.

peans (with the conspicuous exception of France) to adopt such Draconian measures? The answer, apparently, lay in the promised sharing of U.S. energy-related technology. The instrument for technology sharing was the International Energy Agency (IEA).

The IEA originally identified ten areas for R&D cooperation among the IEP signatories:

1. Coal technologies (mining, desulferization, liquifaction, gasification)
2. Solar energy
3. Radioactive waste management
4. Thermonuclear fusion
5. Hydrogen from water
6. Nuclear reactor safety
7. Uses of waste heat
8. Energy conservation
9. Industrial and urban waste utilization
10. Energy systems analysis

Cooperation in geothermal energy was added subsequently. The list raises fascinating questions. Only the first and eighth areas (and less plausibly the seventh and ninth) were relevant to the IEP mission, in that only these offered any near-term hope of easing the social and economic costs inherent in the emergency program. The others, however important, are either decades from realization or deal with social concerns (e.g., reactor safety, radioactive waste management) that surely would not deter necessary political action in the face of a prolonged OPEC–induced energy crisis. Yet the IEP concept is based on success in achieving an efficient international "division of R&D labor" on these items and effective international sharing (among IEP paticipants but not with others) of the innovative results on a scale not previously attempted and for stakes far higher than those in any previous cooperative effort. Consider what is required: international sharing of technological risks, investment risks, and political risks (domestic and international). This clearly implies concertation of national policies and commitment to the unpredictable results of such policies in areas that are unfamiliar (to government officials if not to MNCs) and in ways that may encounter insurmountable domestic political obstacles.

If the burden of R&D labor is to be shared, especially in the face of a potential emergency, nations must be prepared for the risk that a particular approach may not be within the state of the art in the relevant time frame; or may lead to massive cost overruns; or, while demonstrably feasible, may not prove economically competitive in a market made imperfect by the policies of other IEP members or because of the OPEC ability to manipulate the competitive (or, in economic terms, the *upset*) price. The last possibility is obviously real, looming over all the technological options for reducing dependence on imported oil. The internal Saudi Arabian price for wellhead crude, covering all costs, is stable at about $1.50 per barrel. This contrasts with a world market price of about $12.50 per barrel in 1977. Clearly there is ample room for the Saudis, if they choose, to glut the international market with oil at prices that make alternative fuels—especially the exotics, like synthetic fuels from coal—completely uneconomic. The concept of a *safeguard price* for oil, which is now part of the IEA program, is intended to obviate this difficulty. It was set initially at $7 per barrel. The safeguard price concept has two basic weaknesses: First, it is well below the cost of alternative fuels from present or near-term technologies and thus provides no inducement for private investment in alternative technologies; and second, the solidarity of the IEP in the event the Arabs were to drop their oil price below the safeguard level has yet to be tested. The experience, should it happen, will provide a severe test.

Supposing that R&D on the new technologies proves successful, and that means are found to make them acceptable in the face of OPEC oil price flexibility. How will the rights to exploit the most promising technologies by shared among the IEA membership? Will those who put their money into less successful approaches receive equal treatment? How will nonsignatories to IEP/IEA be constrained from reaping the same benefits while having avoided the heavy costs of parallel approaches to a variety of possible technological solutions and the onerous responsibilities of an emergency sharing program? These are not trivial questions, especially in light of the fact that the realization of new technological solutions will have to be carried out in the industrial sector, where the candidate firms are linked by long-standing technology-sharing agreements with IEP/IEA members and nonmembers as well.

The massive transfers of U.S. technology via the IEA that were initially visualized have not occurred. Nonetheless, the IEA and its various working parties have proven to be a valuable forum for information exchange and for developing R&D agendas. The general waning of public perception of the "crisis," together with OPEC moderation, have left the IEP/IEA concept largely untested.

NUCLEAR ENERGY

The development of nuclear power has been heralded by many as the way out of the energy bind. The reason is simple: Using as fuel a reasonably abundant and widely distributed chemical element, nuclear reactors can extract from a few pounds of uranium useful energy equivalent to that contained in thousands of barrels of oil or thousands of tons of coal.

More specifically, if per capita electricity consumption were to continue to grow at 5 percent per year, and petroleum is of necessity reserved for vehicular use and the production of fertilizers and chemicals, U.S. coal production will have to be expanded by a factor of 12 by 2000 A.D. if the "nuclear option" is foregone.[12] The resulting land destruction and stream and water pollution from mining and air pollution from burning—to say nothing of recruiting and training the number of miners required, building the additional railroad trackage and rolling stock, and so on—might prove impossible, politically and economically.

Unfortunately, the widespread use of nuclear reactors raises technological, social, and political problems of major proportions, of which the public is increasingly aware. The impact of these problems is inherently international, and it is the international issues and the technological and political strategies for dealing with them that will be considered here. The discussion will necessarily be brief; but few issues have received greater attention in scholarly publications and the popular media, so those who wish to examine these issues in greater depth will have no difficulty locating material.

The Nuclear Fuel Cycle

Before the public policy issues are addressed, it will be useful to review the principles of nuclear power, since it is the various phases through which natural uranium passes before, during, and after its use in reactors that is the source of the difficulties.

Uranium is naturally radioactive; that is, it spontaneously gives off a variety of elementary (subatomic) particles. When a *critical mass* of uranium is brought together in close proximity, the emitted particles strike the nuclei of adjacent "fertile" atoms with such force that their nuclei are broken apart. This *fission* process releases great amounts of heat energy as well as highly energetic neutrons, which, striking other fertile nuclei, cause them to fission; thus a self-sustaining chain reaction occurs. The heat that is released can be used to create steam for driving turbine generators.

Under very specific circumstances, the rate of nuclear fission can rise exceedingly rapidly and result in an atomic explosion. Fortunately, the circumstances that can produce a nuclear explosion are unique and require particular configurations—not present in power reactors—to achieve. Nuclear reactors can overheat, however, and special design precautions are required to prevent this or to limit the effects if a design failure occurs. The possibility of a nuclear reactor bursting its seams and spewing highly radioactive materials over its surroundings is exceedingly remote, and the risk to public health and safety very small indeed.[13] Nonetheless, since such a catastrophe could not occur at all without nuclear reactors, the moral question involved is a basic one. Since society demands more energy than can reasonably be produced by the other available means, however, and since it routinely accepts much higher risks as part of much less basic functions (e.g., personal automobiles), it is highly likely that the political process will decide to accept the risks involved.

In the simple description of the fission process given above, some important points were omitted. First of all, natural uranium occurs in two isotopes (forms of identical chemical activity but of different mass; the distinction coming from a difference in the number of neutrons in the atomic nucleus). U^{238}, which constitutes 99.3 percent of the natural material, is much more difficult to bring to a chain reaction than U^{235}, with a natural abundance of only 0.7 percent; thus U^{235} is said to be "fertile." Uranium fuel for reactors is, therefore, processed to increase the proportion of U^{235} to perhaps 3 percent. This desired *enrichment* can be obtained by several processes, each of which involves very large capital investments and consumes a great deal of electricity, about one-fifth that eventually produced from the enriched fuel. (It should be noted here, for reference when we get to nuclear proliferation issues, that uranium can be enriched—even to the 60–70 percent levels that yield "weapons grade" material—by a variety of techniques, including centrifuge, gas nozzle, and laser schemes, relatively simply and cheaply, in capital terms—if the quantity desired is not large. In other words, if raw material for a few atomic weapons is the object, rather than economic fuel for a major power reactor program, enrichment is a widely available and relatively cheap technological approach.[14])

Nuclear reactors produce an artificial element, plutonium, as a byproduct. (U^{238} atoms capture one or two neutrons emitted by U^{235} and are transformed into a mixture of plutonium-239 and plutonium-240.) Plutonium itself is highly radioactive—it is the stuff from which modern atomic weapons are made—and highly poisonous as well.

When the reactor fuel elements are *spent*, that is, when the proportion of fissionable fuel has been reduced below the level for efficient reactor operation, they must be replaced. The spent fuel elements must either be securely stored for many years (see later discussion of waste disposal) or must undergo reprocessing, that is, chemical separation of the potentially reusable material from the useless by-products. Reprocessing is intricate, and the radioactive materials must be handled with great care, but the technology is now widely known.[15]

Breeder reactors employ as fuel a mixture of uranium (and sometimes thorium) with plutonium. Their advantage is that they convert nonfissile U^{238} to plutonium or thorium to U^{233} (plutonium and U^{233} are both useful nuclear fuels) at a faster rate than the original fissionable isotopes are consumed, thus *breeding* a surplus of fuel. It is estimated that successful use of breeder reactors would multiply the energy recoverable from natural uranium resources at least fifty times, as contrasted with the once-through fuel cycle of existing light water reactors (LWRs), besides removing the need for additional uranium enrichment facilities. The U.S. Department of Energy and the corresponding authorities in France, Germany, Japan, the United Kingdom, and the U.S.S.R. have spent, and all but the United States are still spending, vast sums on breeder development. However, the U.S. Nuclear Regulatory Commission (which has legal authority in such matters) has not authorized the use in the United States of recycled plutonium as a nuclear fuel, and President Carter in April 1977 extended the previous administration's moratorium on commercialization of reprocessing.

As noted earlier, the technology for chemical separation of plutonium and other useful fissionable materials from spent reactor fuel elements is widely diffused internationally. In fact, the Indians employed it with the spent fuels from a Canadian-supplied research reactor to obtain the plutonium used in their successful test of a "peaceful nuclear device" in May 1974.

Public Policy Issues

The global emergence of the reality of nuclear power and the increased public visibility of some of its critics have led to widespread debate on a number of difficult and interlocking public issues. The nature of nuclear power and of energy politics combine to make these issues international in character. National differences in resource endowments (including technology) and in social goals and priorities insure that the international debate about them reflects deeply divergent interests and perceptions.

In the sections that follow I will take up briefly five main issues: reactor safety and reactor siting; radioactive waste disposal; nuclear proliferation (including the problems of safeguards and physical security measures); the world supply of reactor fuels; and the related questions of a comprehensive ban on tests of nuclear weapons and the role of peaceful nuclear explosives (PNEs).

Reactor Safety   Perhaps the earliest issue to attain widespread public attention was the question of the possible hazards to public health and safety posed by nuclear reactors. "Would you want to live next to one?" scare stories propagated by some critics of the program and the ease with which many people are able to associate the idea of nuclear reactors with the (quite different) concept of atomic bombs have led to widespread concern, particularly among those people who live or work in the neighborhood of proposed reactor sites. Criticisms of the technical adequacy of the AEC Reactor Safety Program by a number of professionally qualified scientists and engineers, combined with the suspicion that the AEC top management was so committed to the"nuclear economy" that it gave short shift to questions of safety, led in 1975 to the restructuring of the AEC into ERDA and the Nuclear Regulatory Commission (NRC), separating the developers from the guardians of broader public interests.* Public interest in safety issues remains high, and because the National Environmental Policy Act provides a remarkably powerful instrument for public participation in this area of policy (see Chapter 2), it is unlikely to diminish. Public perceptions of the technological factors involved have matured, however, and the public safety concern has shifted from a focus on the reactor itself to embrace fuel fabrication and reprocessing facilities, radioactive waste disposal questions, and (belatedly) the public health problems associated with the increased use of coal.

Abroad, public interest in these matters came later than in the United States, as the widespread use of reactors did, but it is no less intensive. Massive antinuclear demonstrations have occurred in West Germany and France, and the nuclear issue defeated a socialist government in Sweden (where five nuclear plants were in operation and seven more ordered). Nuclear reactor safety and radioactive waste disposal were included as items for cooperative R&D in the IEA work plan, primarily to "reduce the public acceptance impediment" to nuclear energy in the European member countries.

_____

* In 1977 ERDA became a part of the new Department of Energy.

Radioactive Waste Disposal Spent nuclear fuel elements are highly radioactive and pose storage or disposal problems of major proportions in both technological and political terms.

The spent fuel material is a mixture of U^{238}, unburned U^{235}, and a variety of intensely radioactive isotopes of cesium, strontium, iodine, and other elements. Chemical separation is indicated before disposal because of the economic value of the material reusable as fuel (although U.S. policy does not permit such use) and in order to concentrate the relatively small proportion of the intensely radioactive "high-level" wastes from the enormous volume of "low-level" wastes involved. A further reduction in volume of about eight to one can be achieved if the high-level waste is dried and fused to a glassy form, with the corollary advantage that in this form the dangerous materials cannot "migrate" to its surroundings.[16]

When both commercial and military wastes are taken into account, the scale of the disposal problem after separation and glassification remains enormous. According to Luther Carter, commenting in *Science* magazine on planned U.S. reactors only:

> If an effective program aimed at permanent disposal is soon initiated, the total volume of solidified waste on hand by the year 2000 could come to 11 million cubic feet, or enough to fill more than 90,000 huge canisters, each one 10 feet in height, 4 feet in diameter, and weighing as much as 8 to 10 tons. In addition, at least 1 million drums of low- to intermediate-level transuranic waste—much of which already has been packaged and buried in a retrievable mode—will have to be committed to repositories.[17]

Low-level wastes can be properly disposed of by burial in deep trenches. Unfortunately, early waste-disposal practices resulted in the burial (or disposal on the sea bed) of large quantities of intermediate-level wastes that cannot be retrieved for disposal by means now recognized as less hazardous.

Disposal of high-level waste means highly isolated repositories protected from human contact or leakage to groundwater and the ecosystem for incredibly long periods of time. On the basis of ERDA data and arbitrarily defining the duration of hazard as the time for a given waste to decay in radioactivity to the same ingestion hazard as that of a rich uranium ore (carnotite), Gene Rochlin has calculated a hazard time ranging from the age of the Pyramids to that of the oldest ocean floor rock.[18] Various depository schemes have been suggested, particularly deep embedment in natural salt domes or deposit on the seabed, that should meet the technical requirement; political solutions remain elusive, however.

The radioactive waste disposal issue is a matter of great public interest, here and abroad. Attempts were made by popular referendum in six U.S. states in 1976 to halt nuclear plant construction until a permanent solution to waste disposal was found; all failed. However, the Swedish parliament wrote such a restriction into law. In a statement just prior to the 1975 election, President Ford said he would speed up the effort to find a suitable method for radioactive waste disposal and directed the Secretary of State to initiate international discussions on the possibility of establishing centrally located multinational waste repositories.[19]

There can be no doubt that the disposal of radioactive waste is a major international political issue. It will be an enduring one. All of humanity has a proper concern with arrangements for insuring the health and safety of all future generations, especially when their institutional aspects are required to endure for a period as long as all of history.

Proliferation of Nuclear Arms   The major international issue created by the spreading use of nuclear power is the proliferation of the potential for building nuclear weapons.* As described earlier, reactors yield plutonium; enough for twenty-five or more Hiroshima-sized bombs is produced annually within the spent fuel rods of a standard 1,000 megawatt power reactor. Enough plutonium for 1,000 bombs a year is now being produced outside the United States and the Soviet Union, a figure that will be tripled in Third World countries alone in the 1980s.[20] The technical significance of these facts is that enormous capital outlays on uranium enrichment facilities are no longer necessary to acquiring the stuff from which nuclear weapons are made, providing someone is willing to supply reactor fuel and the reprocessing chemistry is mastered. As indicated earlier, the technology for chemical separation of the plutonium is readily accessible, and small-scale separation facilities are not especially expensive. The principles for designing an explosive device using plutonium have been generally understood for years. The feasibility of producing a nuclear explosive without recourse to technical assistance from the nuclear powers was dramatically and conclusively demonstrated by India's successful test of a PNE.

---

*It was the development of the means to build nuclear weapons during and immediately following World War II, of course, that started the whole business. It is beyond the scope of this book to describe the attempts of the superpowers to contain their respective *internal* (or what some call *vertical*) proliferations of nuclear weaponry. For a full account see John Newhouse, *Cold Dawn: The Story of SALT.* New York: Holt, Rinehart and Winston, 1973; also Gerald C. Smith, *SALT: The First Strategic Arms Negotiation.* Garden City, N.Y.: Doubleday, 1977.

Philip Farley, a former deputy director of the U.S. Arms Control and Disarmament Agency, has provided a thoughtful summary of current assessments of the international political significance of a spread of nuclear weapons programs.[21] As Farley points out, quite different assessments can be made. One sees a spread in stable deterrence analogous to the U.S.–U.S.S.R. strategic balance. Nuclear proliferation might even enable middle-rank powers to provide minimal nuclear deterrence against the superpowers analogous to the role some claim for British and French nuclear forces. An opposite view foresees an intensification of world and regional tensions, instabilities, and risks, perhaps to catastrophic proportions. Farley points out that uncertainty of consequences is inevitable, in regional situations; in alliances with one or the other of the superpowers, in the risk of accidents, miscalculations, or adventurism.

The United States for years has put principal reliance for containing nuclear proliferation on the Treaty on the Non-Proliferation of Nuclear Weapons (the NPT) of 1963 and the associated Nuclear Safeguards Program of the International Atomic Energy Agency (IAEA).[22] The NPT was largely the creature of the United States and the U.S.S.R., whose national interests in this area, at least, are remarkably congruent. There were in 1976 ninety-five nonnuclear parties to the NPT, plus an additional thirteen signatories who have not yet ratified. However, a number of sensitive or potentially powerful states are not signatories (Argentina, Brazil, Chile, India, Israel, Pakistan, South Africa, and Spain, in addition to France and China) or have not ratified (Egypt, Indonesia, Switzerland, and Turkey). Yet most of these nonparties have publicly declared their acceptance of the principle of peaceful use only, and some give far more than lip service to nonproliferation, including France.

IAEA safeguards and the bilateral safeguards the United States insists on in supplying reactors and fuels to nonparties to the NPT are essentially bookkeeping procedures, based on limited physical audits. The adequacy of these safeguards has been challenged by many experts on technical grounds; but a more serious question, not often enough raised, is: "What would be done if cheating were detected?"

U.S. policy makers have recognized this question. In his 1976 policy statement, President Ford for the first time called for "the immediate imposition of drastic sanctions" in the event of "any material violation of a nuclear safeguards agreement," promising "as a minimum" that the United States would invoke "an immediate cutoff of our supply of nuclear fuel and cooperation." The minimum sanctions President Ford suggested might have little impact on a government intent on developing a nuclear weapons capability, and would have none at all on a terrorist group who might seize the weapons materials (or even an operational weapon). Spokesmen for the Carter administration express the problem differently. They see the purpose of safeguards as giving "a timely warning for diplomacy to work."[23]

The U.S. view is that while the present system of safeguards is adequate to a nuclear economy based on light water reactors, reprocessing and recycling would create proliferation possibilities that make the present safeguards ineffective. The warning time would be too short. The Carter administration nuclear policy, building on Ford's, would forgo reprocessing and recycling and the breeder reactor domestically and would not export these technologies. Recognizing that reprocessing technology is already widely diffused,* U.S. officials are still hopeful that the U.S. example will cause other nations to defer their reprocessing and breeder reactor plans at least until a thorough international review of alternative safeguardable fuel cycles can be accomplished. (I will analyze U.S. policy and international reactions to it later.)

Uranium Reserves and Assured Fuel Supplies   A nuclear economy—even as a "last resort" (in President Carter's language) transition to an economy based on "inexhaustible" energy resources—is technologically and politically credible only to the extent that the availability of sufficient reactor fuel at acceptable costs is assured (in both absolute and autarkic terms). Basically, reactor fuel availability depends on two factors: the technological-economic dimension hinges on the relationship between world ore reserves and prices; the political dimension reflects the fact that only a very limited number of suppliers offer enrichment services to the world market. These are the United States, the Soviet Union, URENCO (the Netherlands, the United Kingdom, and West Germany centrifuge project), and EURODIF (a joint venture of France—with financial participation from Iran—Belgium, Italy, and Spain). Neither of the latter two organizations will make quantity deliveries before 1979.

The question of ore reserves—U.S. and foreign—is the subject of hot debate, characterized by widely varying estimates of future availability at various prices. The U.S. mining industry has spent upward of $50 million per year on exploration for more than a decade ($157 million was forecast for 1976[24]), but new ore field finds are

---

* At least six nations have demonstrated the technology to a pilot scale: the United States, the U.S.S.R., France, Germany, the United Kingdom, and India. Japan, Taiwan, and Israel are known to have laboratory capabilities. Germany has agreed to provide Brazil with a full-scale plant.

only a part of the story. It takes seven or eight years to bring a new discovery to production, and capital costs are rising. Recent volatility of the spot price on which the necessarily long-term contracts are written ($10 to $41 per pound between 1973 and 1976), constantly shifting estimates of future energy demand, and technological and political uncertainties about the fuel cycles likely to be employed combine to create great uncertainties about the uranium supply future.[25] In particular, many people abroad note that President Carter's decision to defer the U.S. fuel reprocessing and breeder programs depends on assumptions regarding uranium availability that may be sound for the United States but would not be defensible for most other nations.

As indicated, the question of enrichment capacity is every bit as confusing as the amount of uranium available for enrichment. Both technological and political factors are involved. All present large enrichment plants, worldwide, are based on the gaseous diffusion process evolved during World War II. Current U.S. thinking, like that of the URENCO partners, leans to centrifuge technology. South Africa is building a full-scale plant based (presumably) on gas nozzle technology. The possibility of laser separation techniques looms on the horizon.[26] The choice involves major uncertainties regarding both capital and operating costs. The economic capacity of any plant depends also on the question of "tails assay," that is, the proportion of the fertile isotope U^{235} that remains in the unenriched residue. More useful fuel can be produced by a particular plant as the tails assay is lowered, but the cost of incremental production rises rapidly.*

The political complications of the enrichment question are more resistant to "scientific" solutions. There is, first of all, the unanimous desire of the nuclear weapons states to curtail the global proliferation of enrichment capabilities. They see their motivation as a concern with global political-military stability. Some of the nonweapons states see other, more devious, motivations, particularly in light of the U.S. near-monopoly on world enriched uranium available for export. States with enrichment capabilities understandably will insure adequate fuel for their domestic needs before contracting for its export. This is viewed by others as leading them to unacceptable dependence on possibly unreliable foreign suppliers for a material critical to their economic well-being and political independence. (It is this concern that has led so many of them to the view that domestic fuel reprocessing and recycling are crucial to their futures.)

---

*The tails assay of the very large amounts of residuals from uranium already processed by U.S. enrichment plants for civil and military programs remains relatively high compared with what would currently be regarded as economic. These tails are one of the largest proven uranium reserves in the world.

President Carter's nuclear power policy offers fuel guarantees, but only to those who agree to forgo reprocessing and recycling. I will say more on this later, but first it is necessary to identify one more area of international disagreement that further complicates the problem.

Weapons Test Bans and Peaceful Nuclear Explosives   The International Atomic Energy Agency (IAEA) was created in 1957 as an autonomous body closely associated with the UN.[27] Growing out of increasing international concern with the safeguarding of nuclear materials that might be used to produce weapons on the one hand, and with diffusing the benefits of peaceful applications to the nonweapons states on the other, the IAEA efforts quickly became entangled with most of the matters already mentioned and with two others as well: nuclear weapons test bans and the possibilities of peaceful nuclear explosives.

Both questions arose from the activities of the weapons powers, particularly the United States and the U.S.S.R. Interest in curbing the enormously expensive and dangerous arms race led these two countries, along with the United Kingdom, to sign a limited test ban treaty in 1963. This treaty banned all nuclear weapons tests except those conducted underground; it failed to deal effectively with PNEs, with which both the United States and the U.S.S.R. were experimenting. These three nations also took the lead in the UN General Assembly in pushing the development of the Treaty on Non-Proliferation of Nuclear Weapons, which was signed by fifty-three countries on July 1, 1968. The major inducements for adherence offered to the nonweapons states were the promise of access to "peaceful nuclear technologies," including PNEs, and the commitment by the weapons states to aggressively seek a comprehensive test ban treaty. In fact, a comprehensive test ban treaty does not yet exist, in part because of the complications introduced by the PNE aspect.* Another reason, of course, is that powerful military interests in each nuclear weapons state remain opposed to limitations on the development and verification of new weapons designs. There remains, too, the problem of acceptance of such a ban by others, particularly the People's Republic of China.

The United States spent cumulatively about $160 million on PNE experiments beginning in the late 1950s. Technological disillusionment set in, however, and when the citizens of Colorado amended

---

*The Carter administration continues to energetically seek such a treaty.

their state's constitution to effectively ban further PNE tests there, the U.S. PNE program was abandoned in 1975.[28] Soviet interest remains high, however, bolstered by rhetorical references to the NPT commitments of technical assistance to the nonnuclear powers.

There is no technological basis for distinguishing between a test (or even an operational use) of a PNE and a test of a nuclear warhead. It was recognition of this fact, as it related to the Indian test in 1974, that led the United States to adopt a policy that denies the use of any U.S.–supplied nuclear materials or facilities in *any* form of nuclear explosive.

Domestic and world pressures for movement toward a comprehensive test ban treaty continued, but the Soviets steadfastly refused to consider a treaty that would force abandonment of PNEs. The resulting compromise was two companion treaties. The first, the Limited Test Ban Treaty of 1974, set a limit of 150 kilotons on any single explosion, including PNEs. The domestic arms control community and much of world opinion have regarded this as miniscule progress toward a comprehensive test ban. The companion agreement, however, the Treaty on Underground Nuclear Explosions for Peaceful Purposes (PNET) of 1976, offers greater promise and is certainly one of the most technologically complex international protocols ever negotiated.[29] Recognizing that the remote monitoring technologies relied on for policing compliance with the Limited Test Ban are insufficient to the PNE situation (particularly when PNEs are fired in salvos, a possibility much prized by the Soviets), the PNET provides exceedingly detailed prescriptions for on-site inspection.

The principle of on-site inspection has always been uppermost in the minds of U.S. arms control strategists; it has always been firmly rejected by the Soviets. The PNET may represent the breakthrough needed to open the way for a comprehensive test ban. As of late 1977 the Soviets have announced their willingness to agree to a limited moratorium on PNEs, thus offering new hope on the possibility of a comprehensive test ban.

U.S. Nuclear Policy and Its International Implications

As mentioned above, just prior to the 1976 elections President Ford announced a new policy that backed away from earlier plans to recycle plutonium as a reactor fuel. "The U.S. should no longer regard the reprocessing of nuclear fuel as a necessary and inevitable step," the President said. Reprocessing and recycling should be permitted "if they are found to be consistent with our international objectives." The effects of existing foreign reprocessing facilities were not addressed.

President Ford further called upon all countries to refrain from exporting reprocessing technology or uranium enrichment plants for at least three years, and directed the initiation of discussions with other suppliers to seek arrangements for coordinating fuel services. Ford further directed the Secretary of State to undertake international talks aimed at establishing a new facility for storing plutonium and spent fuel under the control of IAEA.

In a series of statements in April 1977, President Carter enunciated a comprehensive energy plan that picked up, in the portions dealing with the nuclear fuel cycle, President Ford's earlier propositions but developed them much further. President Carter's policy derives from several basic concerns:

- The belief that nuclear power is an essential element of the U.S. and world energy economy for at least the next quarter century.
- A possible major threat to world peace and stability from the spread of nuclear weapons capabilities to nonweapons states and the threat that these capabilities might come into the hands of terrorist groups.
- The conclusion that present international and bilateral safeguards, while adequate to the "front end" of the nuclear fuel cycle (i.e., to the fueling of LWRs), are *not* adequate to the "back end" (i.e., reprocessing, plutonium separation, and recycling).
- The conviction that more safeguardable fuel cycles can be devised if the international community adopts that as a high-priority objective.

The stated goal of President Carter's policy, as regards the nuclear proliferation threat, is to insure that "diplomacy will have time to work" if a diversion of nuclear material to a weapons or explosives (the two are equated for policy purposes) program is detected. The policy, contained in presidential statements made in April 1977 and in legislation proposed to the Congress in that same month, is a "package" containing the following key elements:

- Indefinite deferral of commercial reprocessing and plutonium recycling in the United States.

- Deferral of the date U.S. breeder reactors would come on-line, and reorientation of the U.S. breeder program to the exploration of "proliferation-resistant" fuel cycles.
- Embargoing of U.S. exports of enrichment and reprocessing technologies.
- Tightening of safeguards in new bilateral agreements for cooperation (including the provision of reactors and enriched fuel) and the extension of safeguards to *all* nuclear equipment and materials, wherever originated, in the recipient country.
- Renegotiation of existing bilateral cooperation agreements to bring them in line with the terms of new agreements.
- New U.S. enriched fuel guarantees for those NPT signatories who forgo processing.
- U.S. agreement to interim (and perhaps permanent) storage of radioactive wastes from U.S.–fueled reactors abroad.

In February 1978 Congress passed the Nuclear Non-Proliferation Act of 1978, embodying all the elements cited above (although influential congresspeople continue to resist President Carter's efforts to cancel the Clinch River breeder reactor demonstration project).[30] One provision of the act—that all agreements covering U.S. supply of reactor fuels should provide also that reprocessing of those fuels would require U.S. approval on a case-by-case basis—has provoked intense negative reaction abroad.

In support of his policy objectives, President Carter proposed the creation of an International Nuclear Fuel Cycle Evaluation Program (INFCE) to undertake cooperative analyses of the proliferation potentials associated with current and projected nuclear fuel cycles and the possibilities for more proliferation-resistant fuel cycle alternatives for new reactor designs. Over fifty nations are participating in the project, which began in October 1977; it is expected that analytical work will be completed within two years.[31]

Both foreign and domestic reactions to the U.S. policies and legislation have been, initially at least, vocal and preponderantly negative. While no one will disavow the central goal of the program—nonproliferation—many critics argue that the measures adopted are unworkable or unnecessary (or both) in achieving that end. The policy's underlying assumptions with regard to the availability of uranium at acceptable prices are widely challenged. As indicated earlier, many foreign nations are committed to the view that only reprocessing and recycling can assure them an acceptable degree of national energy independence.

Domestic critics of the policy point to the poor condition of the U.S. nuclear industry as regards new orders and blame the President and the Congress for creating an environment of uncertainty and resentment. Some foreign critics claim to see in the U.S. policy a desire for commercial domination of the world market for both reactors and fuels.

What now appears to be U.S. intransigence in the face of basic international concerns hopefully will, in time, come to be seen as evidence of President Carter's willingness to assert U.S. leadership for the international community in facing up to basic intractable realities that most politicians would as soon overlook. The practical political question of whether the support of moral principle in the pursuit of international agreement is a workable strategy remains unresolved. Perhaps it will always be thus.

Notes

1. For valuable compendia of recent analytical studies of global food supply that profusely illustrate the bewildering interplay of economics, land use, water resources, energy and fertilizer requirements, the bureaucratic proclivities of national and international governmental organizations, and much more, see special issues of *New Scientist* (London), November 7, 1974, **64**; *Science*, May 9, 1975, **188**; and *Scientific American*, September 1976, **235**. For a basic reference see Schlomo Reutlinger and Marcelo Selowsky, *Malnutrition and Poverty*. Baltimore, Md.: Johns Hopkins University Press, 1976; also Dan Morgan, Growing World Food Gap Seen if Policies Unchanged. Washington (D.C.) *Post*, October 21, 1974—a particularly illuminating report of the conflict in policy approach between Secretary Kissinger and Secretary Butz on the eve of the UN World Food Conference.

2. Terence Price provides a thoughtful overview in his General Introduction to the *Proceedings of the NATO Conference on a Strategy for Resources*, 1975, Eindhoven, the Netherlands.

3. Connelly, Philip, and Perlinan, Robert. *The Politics of Scarcity: Resource Conflicts in International Relations*. Oxford: Oxford University Press, 1975. See also Edward R. Fried and Philip H. Trezise, The United States in the World Economy. In Henry Owen and Charles L. Schultze (eds.), *Setting National Priorities: The Next Ten Years*. Washington, D.C.: The Brookings Institution, 1976.

4. For a fascinating attempt to bridge the two points of view see Mihajlo Mesarovic and Edward Pestel, *Mankind at the Turning Point*. New York: Dutton, 1974.

5. These issues are discussed in depth in Connelly and Perlinan, *The Politics of Scarcity*.

6. *International Trade, 1974–75.* Geneva: General Agreement on Tariffs and Trade, 1976, Table E. No possibility of a serious disruption of the world economy by a politically motivated embargo, such as that imposed on oil exports by the OPEC countries in 1974, is suggested by any aspect of current trade patterns. Greater price stability, on the other hand, would be welcome to producers and consumers alike (the degree of welcome accorded by each would depend on the price at which stability occurred, of course). Various proposals directed to that goal have been put forward at the 1976 UNCTAD Conference in Nairobi and at other forums. For a summary and the present U.S position on each see the *International Economic Report of the President, 1976.* Washington, D.C.: Council on International Economic Policy, p. 91ff.

7. Colombo, Umberto. *Problems of Materials Resources.* Paris: Organisation for Economic Co-operation and Development, 1974, Paper SPT (74) 7. Dr. Colombo notes the immense amount of critical metals contained in scrapped automobiles. Recent data show that for the United States alone more than 8 million cars, trucks, and buses are scrapped or abandoned annually, representing 10 million tons of steel, 100 thousand tons of copper, 175 thousand tons of lead, and 2 million tons each of zinc and aluminum. The energy involved in initial production and in recycling of scrap is obviously very large.

8. Fried, Edward R., and Schultze, Charles L., eds. *Higher Oil Prices and the World Economy.* Washington, D.C.: The Brookings Institution, 1975.

9. Fried and Schultze, *Higher Oil Prices.*

10. Nau, Henry. U.S. Foreign Policy in the Energy Crisis. *Atlantic Community Quarterly,* Winter 1974-1975, **12,** 426–439.

11. Ray, Dixy Lee. *The Nation's Energy Future: A Report to the President of the United States.* Washington, D.C.: Atomic Energy Commission, Doc. No. WASH–1281, 1973.

12. Minnick, Lawrence, and Murphy, Mike. The Breeders: When and Why. *EPRI Journal,* March 1976.

13. *Reactor Safety Study: An Assessment of Accident Risks in U.S. Commercial Nuclear Power Plants* (The Rasmussen Report). Washington, D.C.: Nuclear Regulatory Commission, Doc. No. NUREG–75/014, 1975.

14. Bebbington, William P. The Reprocessing of Nuclear Fuels. *Scientific American,* December 1976, **235,** 30ff.

15. *Report to the American Physical Society by the Study Group on Nuclear Fuel Cycles and Waste Management.* Washington, D.C.: American Physical Society, 1977, Chapter 6.

16. Dan, Gary, and Williams, Robert. Secure Storage of Radioactive Waste. *EPRI Journal,* July–August 1976.

17. Carter, Luther J. The Radioactive Waste Inventory. *Science,* 1977, **195,** 662; and Radioactive Wastes: Some Urgent Unfinished Business, *Science,* 1977, **195,** 661ff.

18. Rochlin, Gene I. Nuclear Wastes Disposal: Two Social Criteria. *Science,* 1977, **195,** 23ff. See also Bernard L. Cohen, The Disposal of Radioactive Wastes from Fission Reactors. *Scientific American,* June 1977, **236,** 21–31.

19. Ford, Gerald S. Statement by the President on Nuclear Policy. Washington, D.C.: October 28, 1976. Related remarks were included by the President in a speech of that date in Cincinnati, Ohio.

20. Congressional Research Service. *Facts on Nuclear Proliferation: A Handbook.* Washington, D.C.: Senate Committee on Government Operations, 1975.

21. Farley, Philip J. Nuclear Proliferation. In Henry Owen and Charles L. Schultze (eds.), *Setting National Priorities: The Next Ten Years.* Washington, D.C.: The Brookings Institution, 1976, pp. 129–166.

22. See *Facts on Nuclear Proliferation.* See also *Safeguards.* Vienna: International Atomic Energy Agency, 1973; and Treaty on the Non-Proliferation of Nuclear Weapons; Review Conference, May 1975. *International Atomic Energy Agency Bulletin,* 1975, **17,** No. 2.

23. Nye, Joseph S. Statement given at the International Conference on Nuclear Power and Its Fuel Cycle, Salzburg, Austria, May 2, 1977. Department of State *Bulletin,* May 30, 1977, 550–54.

24. Chow, Brian G. The Economic Issues of the Fast Breeder Reactor Program. *Science,* 1977, **195,** 551ff.

25. The Uranium Future. *The Economist,* January 22–28, 1977.

26. Krass, Allen S. Laser Enrichment of Uranium: The Weapons Proliferation Connection. *Science,* 1977, **196,** 721ff. provides a current assessment of the technology and a thoughtful analysis of its potential impact on nuclear weapons proliferation.

27. Congressional Research Service. Nuclear Weapons Proliferation and the International Atomic Energy Agency. Washington, D.C.: Senate Committee on Government Operations, 1976. This source provides a thorough background.

28. Carter, Luther J. Peaceful Nuclear Explosions: Promises, Promises. *Science,* 1975, **188,** 996.

29. Shapley, Deborah. Nuclear Explosives: Technology for On-Site Inspection. *Science,* 1976, **193,** 743.

30. For a detailed exposition of the Carter administration policy by one of its principal architects, see Joseph S. Nye, Nonproliferation: A Long-Term Strategy. *Foreign Affairs,* April 1978.

31. For greater detail on the plans and expectations for INFCE see Nye, Nonproliferation.

8

TECHNOLOGY AND NATIONAL SOVEREIGNTY

Some applications of technology offering great potential benefits to many nations also have the potential for inequitable impacts or for misuse in ways that would incur disproportionate social costs. When the scope of their implementation and their social and economic impact is, inherently or by mandate, confined to a national territory, the challenge to public policy can be dealt with by national approaches. Not all technologies can be dealt with by national action, however. Some can be implemented only by concerted international action; others have transnational costs and benefits of such proportions that individual nations are unwilling to see them employed by others to the possible disadvantage of their own interests. Unilateral implementation of such technologies thus poses a possible threat to national sovereignty. Collective implementation, on the other hand, may require the surrender of authority to a supranational institution.

EXTRATERRITORIALITY

The extraterritorial extension of one nation's authority into the jurisdiction of another nation, whether by mutual agreement or unilaterally and without recourse, is a common enough aspect of history. The international community has for many years accepted the im-

155

munity from domestic law of accredited foreign diplomats, for example, compromising the limits of national sovereignty in the interest of quid pro quo. There are numerous instances in which a nation's technology policies impose limitations on the behavior of its citizens or corporations in another country that may be inconsistent with the laws of that country. While extraterritoriality per se is not the emphasis of this chapter, it is important to understand the nature of extraterritoriality issues and the international debates they have provoked. I will illustrate with two examples.

One instance already alluded to in Chapter 6 has to do with the extraterritorial application of antitrust laws and other legislation dealing with restrictive business practices. U.S. law prohibits U.S. firms and their foreign subsidiaries from entering into market-division agreements, pricing agreements, and the like with other U.S. or foreign firms that could have the effect of restricting competition or otherwise injuring consumer interests in *U.S.*domestic and import trade. To understand the extraterritorial implications, it is necessary to note three points: First, this U.S. law governs the behavior of business enterprises operating in, and staffed by nationals of, another country; the ability to assert this jurisdiction rests solely on the fact of management control of the foreign firm by a U.S.–based corporation or partnership. (All of the shares of the foreign firm might be held by U.S. citizens, but so long as no U.S. business entity has effective management control of the foreign enterprise, these U.S. laws are not effective.) Second, the behavior of the foreign enterprise proscribed by these U.S. laws may be entirely legal insofar as the host country is concerned and, in fact, may be actively encouraged by host country policies. Third, the test on which the penalties prescribed by these laws hinges is damage to the interests of U.S. consumers; damage to the interests of the host country are not a consideration.

Understandably, foreign governments regard such U.S. laws (they exist in several areas involving technology-based business activity) as an unjustifiable intrusion into their political sovereignty, and inequitable as regards their economic interests vis-à-vis U.S. economic interests.

A second example of extraterritoriality can be found in U.S. policy on nuclear energy (see Chapter 7). It was pointed out that President Carter's policy would require that a foreign nation place all of its nuclear materials and facilities under international (IAEA) safeguards as a condition for continuing to receive U.S. fuel supplies for its power reactors. Note that *all* in this instance includes not only nuclear equipment and materials that may have been purchased from third countries without such conditions, but also equipment that may have been designed and built from indigenous technology and the nuclear material created by the operation of such "home-grown" facilities. Since the United States is in a near-monopoly position in supplying reactor fuel to the international market, this policy, too, is perceived by many abroad as an unwarranted extraterritorial extension of U.S. policy.

As both of these examples illustrate, the domestic interests that these U.S. policies intend to serve are entirely defensible. The difficulty is that they can come into conflict with the domestic policies of other governments that, in their context, are equally defensible. Alas, international interdependence is no rose garden.

JURISDICTION OVER TECHNOLOGY

Just as some political laws take on extraterritoriality, physical laws and some of their embodiments in technology know no political constraints.

Some technological innovations elude the reach of the body politic. For any or a combination of reasons—the universality of physical principles (which may be imperfectly understood at the time of choice), inadequacies of national and international legal instruments and structures, or unanticipated or unappreciated secondary impacts—the consequences of the application of certain technologies are not confined to national areas. Vested interests in their exploitation (unrecognized or unchallenged in the political arena or initially accepted as undiluted public goods) may operate to suppress public concern or political debate. Some technological impacts accrue cumulatively over periods of time that exceed the sensitivity of scientific monitoring or, more often, the time frames characteristic of political organization and action. (As Chapter 9 brings out, the last point takes on particular relevance in the international domain, since the tenure of heads of state—those generally held responsible for foreign policy matters—is usually much shorter than the political tenure of bureaucrats or even of the leaders of legislative bodies.)

Some examples of important technological applications sharing these characteristics will illustrate their breadth and increasing significance:

- Emerging technologies for exploitation of the living and mineral resources of the deep oceans, at rates well beyond those at which nature replenishes them and in circumstances that disproportionately favor the technologically and economically advanced nations and, of course, the coastal states.[1]

- The applications of satellite technology to direct television broadcasting, applications that do not and cannot recognize political jurisdictions and that give those nations capable of deploying such systems and exploiting their capabilities unprecedented opportunities to transcend the effective authorities of foreign governments.[2]

- The linking by public telecommunications services of privately operated data services and such "invisible" transactions as electronics funds transfer among commercial banks, raising important questions about "data havens," personal rights of privacy and public rights of access to information.[3]

- Environmental pollution and *inadvertant* weather modification, where effects originated by private or public activities in one nation may adversely and uncontrollably affect the well-being of the peoples of another.[4]

- Rainmaking and *deliberate* modification of the natural behavior of typhoons and hurricanes, where operations conducted in the interests of one nation (or of constituencies within it) may affect the essential interests of another, without recourse.

To explore each of these examples in any detail would exhaust the resources of both author and reader. The essential points can be illustrated by examination of two representative instances: the use of satellites for earth resources surveys and weather modification.

Landsat

The Earth Resources Survey Satellite, or Landsat as it is now called, was conceived and developed jointly by the U.S. National Aeronautics and Space Administration and the Department of the Interior. A pair of satellites yields, every nine days, reasonably detailed multispectral images covering virtually all of the earth's surface, subject to the limitations of cloud cover and to the suitable positioning of ground receiving terminals.* Ground terminals, operated by the re-

---

*A videotape recorder carried in the satellite accumulates all the data for a single quasi-polar orbit and "dumps" it at high speed to a particular ground receiver on command. Multiple ground terminals extend this capability to all longitudes. They also make possible direct reception (without reliance on the satellite recorder) of data covering that part of the earth's surface viewed by the satellite during the time it is within line-of-sight range of the ground receiver.

spective national authorities, were in place in 1976 in the United States (two), Canada, Brazil, Chile, Italy, Zaire, and Iran. It is established U.S. policy that photographic reproduction of any or all of these images (whether received by U.S. or foreign-based ground terminals) is available to anyone for a modest fee.

Landsat has been widely acclaimed as a breakthrough in our ability to obtain detailed and comprehensive knowledge of the geological structure of the earth; its river systems, lakes and oceans; and the distribution patterns of forests, buildings, and the like. Using sophisticated computer-assisted analysis techniques, scientists have used Landsat data (usually supplemented by "ground truth" data from other sources) to locate promising mineral deposits, chart the seasonal flooding patterns of river basins and the desertification of arid lands, forecast the yield of food crops and observe the spread of crop diseases, locate regions of ocean upwelling that hold promise for commercial fishing, and dozens of other important matters.

Not all the reactions to this new source of data are enthusiastic. A number of countries, including Brazil, India, and the Soviet Union, have objected to the uncontrolled availability of Landsat data as an infringement of national sovereignty. It is argued that the enormously greater resources for data analysis and for the exploitation of the data for economic purposes that exist in the United States and other technologically advanced countries threaten national control of the LDCs' natural resources. The ability to observe patterns of crop production and to predict yields is seen also as giving the United States (the world's largest exporter of cereal grains) a monopoly advantage in setting world food prices. In fact, the United States has inaugurated a Large Area Crop Inventory Experiment (LACIE) that uses Landsat data as a basis for wheat production forecasts. Its results are published immediately as they become available. These issues have been extensively debated in the Outer Space Committee of the UN General Assembly, and its Science and Technology and Legal subcommittees.[5] International concensus remains illusive.[6]

It has been suggested that the cause of these problems might be eliminated by technological measures. The ground areas actually observed by the satellite could, in principle, be confined by a combined programed masking of the field of view of the satillite-borne sensors and start–stop timing of the recording device to those nations who have agreed in advance to such observations. However, the realization of this concept would involve enormous technological complexity (necessarily entailing some sacrifice of the performance and reliability of the system). Moreover, it would require a degree of faith in the designers of the spacecraft no different in character or degree from faith in U.S. assertions of its intent not to use for unilateral advantage its first access to the satellite data or its superior technology for extracting valuable information from the satellite images.

Another "solution," popular in the UN, is to create (necessarily with U.S. assistance) an international center for the processing and interpretation of Landsat data where, presumably, national preferences about its dissemination would be respected.[7] A more sensible and more useful approach would be for such an international capability to focus on training all comers in the processing and interpretation of Landsat data and in techniques for collating it with other data available from domestic or international sources, so as to maximize Landsat's contributions to specific tasks that have national priority.

The difficulties posed by the restricted availability of Landsat data are largely illusory. The potential benefits of this new data-gathering resource to those who apply them to their own special interests are obvious. It is equally obvious that different users will have different interests and that these interests will conflict from time to time. The special advantages of the advanced countries with respect to the use of Landsat data are partly technological (and will erode with time and the increasing experience of other users), but largely economic; however, in the long run improved information about their own resource endowments will be a greater advantage to the LDCs.

Weather Modification

The deliberate intervention in the natural processes that determine weather and climate had its beginnings in laboratory experiments a quarter of a century ago, when scientists demonstrated that the "seeding" of simulated clouds by small quantities of dry ice or silver oxide could initiate precipitation. Within a few years entrepreneurs were seeding clouds from aircraft or ground-based "burners" for a price—a price willingly paid by farmers, ranchers, and hydroelectric utilities, for whom any promise of relieving the impact of below-normal precipitation had an economic appeal.

These first operations were conducted more or less haphazardly, with comparable results. Carefully organized and scientifically controlled experiments were outside the interests of the customers. Nonetheless, increasing complaints from those who felt they were being robbed of their atmospheric water rights and from customers who felt they had not gotten their money's worth ultimately rose above Washington's customary background noises, and a President's Advisory Committee on Weather Control was established in 1953 to determine "the extent to which the U.S. should experiment with, engage in, or regulate activities designed to control weather conditions." The committee's conclusions, published in 1957, were that a real effect—perhaps an average increase of 10–15 percent in precipitation—was possible, but that greatly expanded research was indicated. While the Congress did not release the desired funds, it did charge the National Science Foundation with the responsibility for supporting the development of the necessary scientific base.

Meanwhile, other countries were not idle. Weather modification experiments were initiated in France, Australia, Brazil, China, Israel, and the U.S.S.R. The goals of the enterprise were expanded beyond precipitation augmentation to include fog dispersal, hail and lightning suppression, and the moderation of severe storms.

The last possibility was recognized very early, and field trials were quickly organized. Effects were clearly evident, but whether they were related to the cloud seeding was not known. In the intervening years, scientists who had turned to the newly available large-scale digital computers in an attempt to examine the dynamic processes of the global atmosphere had produced initial theoretical results that lent credence to the hypothesis that selective seeding of severe tropical storms—hurricanes and typhoons—could indeed reduce their maximum wind velocities. The importance of this possibility to tropical coastal regions is potentially very great indeed. In 1969 a single storm, Hurricane Camille, did $1.4 billion of property damage and took 300 lives on the U.S. Gulf Coast. The typhoon that sent a storm surge from the Bay of Bengal over East Pakistan in 1970 took an estimated 250,000 lives. The U.S. Weather Bureau, in cooperation with U.S. Navy scientists, began experiments with hurricane modification in 1961, and Project Stormfury, a joint program of hurricane research, was formally inaugurated in 1962 and has continued ever since, except for funding interruptions. The results to date have generally supported the early promise. Field experimentation has been limited, however, by a variety of considerations including budget strictures, the shortage of appropriate aircraft, and, most especially, rising concerns about the international political implications of experimentation with severe storms that might, whether or not manipulated, strike various Caribbean nations (read Cuba).

Technological progress in weather modification, which has been based largely on empirical studies, has now reached the point where reasonably predictable and useful results can be obtained in a number of important applications. There is no existing technique, however, for producing rainfall when no clouds are present or for reliably stimulating rainfall from the clouds that most often occur over areas that suffer chronic shortages of rainfall. Rainmaking may in time prove to be economically important, particularly to maintaining yields in agricultural areas that currently suffer from occasional poor seasons, but it cannot be regarded as a panacea—even potentially—for dealing with the problems of chronic drought.

Local weather and climate are, or course, manifestations of a single complex global pattern of atmospheric circulation, energized by the sun and profoundly influenced by physical and chemical interactions with land masses, the oceans, and the polar ice packs. Any human intervention in these processes, therefore, has global implications, at least in principle. It is possible that even localized interventions may produce measurable effects over a much wider area. Scientific understanding of the extent to which this may be true is rudimentary, but there is enough to lend tacit encouragement to the view widely held by governments that manmade interventions in weather processes can have transborder, perhaps (in a few situations) persistent, consequences. Concern with the possibility of such consequences is an active foreign relations issue. In a number of instances, countries have raised the possibility that rainmaking programs conducted by governments or by private operators in adjoining nations may adversely affect their own territory by diminishing the amount of precipitation they receive or by producing undesired excess precipitation.

A related issue, which arises with increasing frequency, is how to deal with the requests received by the technologically advanced countries, especially the United States, for assistance in mounting precipitation augmentation programs in other countries, particularly those affected by drought conditions. The only government-controlled operational capabilities that might be employed in responding to those requests are military, a fact that raises potential international relations problems of its own. Private contractors who possess the requisite capabilities exist, but the requesting country frequently lacks the technical expertise to recognize what capabilities are required and to evaluate proposals from the private sector for such services. A more basic difficulty lies in the fact that the requesting countries seldom possess the expertise in meteorological science to evaluate objectively either the potential success of such a program or, after the fact, the actual results of a seeding program. (Unfortunately, in many of the most serious situations, the problems created by temporary drought simply make visible the basic fact that local water usage requirements exceed a level that is sustainable without major changes in water management programs.) This form of technical assistance, at first sight so easy to provide and in every case so difficult to refuse, can easily be counterproductive to friendly foreign relations.

United States involvement in foreign weather modification programs raises another international political issue. Some people, here and abroad, believe that a principal reason for U.S. investment in the development of this technology is its potential as a weapon of war, even (in the case of hurricane or typhoon modification) as a weapon of mass destruction.[8] While the use of weather modification as a weapon (e.g., stimulating massive flooding of enemy-held territory to interdict troop movements) is conceptually feasible in particular circumstances, those circumstances are determined by global, regional, and local natural weather patterns and not by military strategy. Weather modification is thus a very limited "weapon of opportunity." Nonetheless, some military planners resisted acceptance of a threshold ban on "hostile uses." However, Secretary of State Cyrus Vance signed the Convention on the Prohibition of Military or Any Other Hostile Uses of Environmental Modification Techniques on May 18, 1977.

Progress in the development of techniques for modifying severe tropical storms raises very difficult international issues. If the objectives of this research are realized, it will become possible to reduce substantially the frightful toll of life and property due to typhoons and hurricanes. This enormously important potential benefit is not without equally important potential problems, even though analyses show that the direct costs of conducting such operations would be small compared to the reduction in property loss. The major problems arise, in part, because storm seeding alters the precipitation patterns of the storms and may actually decrease the total amount of rain falling on land areas along the path of the storm. For those land areas near the major centers of severe tropical storm activity (the Gulf of Mexico and the Caribbean, the Western Pacific and the China Sea, and the Bay of Bengal), a significant proportion of total annual rainfall—perhaps one-third to one-half—is associated with hurricanes and typhoons. It might be possible for individual nations to choose between reducing storm damage or maintaining the rainfall vital to agriculture within their own territory, though the political feasibility of making such a choice has never been put to the test. It would be much harder for a number of nations, all potentially affected by the same seasonal storm patterns and often by the same individual storms, to agree on policies for managing an operational capability for modifying severe storms. This is particularly true in light of the following facts: Some will be better equipped than others to minimize storm damage by other means; some are more dependent than others on storm-associated precipitation; some will be better able than others to develop and mount the operational capabilities involved in seeding operations; and, finally, the affected nations will rank each of these considerations differently.

An operational capability for seeding severe tropical storms would have to be used in accordance with internationally agreed guidelines that take into account the differing interests and priorities of the potentially affected nations. It may be necessary that the modification of such storms be under the direct control of some competent supranational body. It is not at all clear how these requirements can be met. Certainly no existing international institutions possess both the necessary technical expertise and the political authority to discharge competently the responsibilities involved. Even an institutional model is lacking. Before such a body could be created, and certainly before it could function effectively, detailed analysis and extensive legal discussions would be required, and a binding international treaty would have to be agreed among the affected nations.

INSTITUTIONAL PROBLEMS

Dealing with the international political challenges posed by technological applications such as Landsat, weather modification, and the other examples mentioned earlier, is a new challenge to the community of nations. Clearly, if there are solutions, they will have to be identified and implemented by collective action. While advanced countries can and must provide leadership in this effort, in today's world no country—not even the United States—has the power to impose an international solution. International organizations, perhaps of a type not yet conceived let alone achieved, will be the essential modality for collective action. The characteristics of international organizations and the politics of using them are the subject of Chapter 9. At this juncture I will look at the requirements for workable collective solutions to the kinds of international technological issues illustrated above.

The first requirement for solution of these issues is obvious. The citizens of all nations, and the public officials who serve as their surrogates, must be informed about the issues and about the technological, economic, and social factors that create them and constrain the choice of solutions. In itself this is not an easy task. The world scientific and technological communities and their international institutions, such as the International Council of Scientific

Unions (ICSU) and the International Institute for Applied Systems Analysis (IIASA), have a major responsibility and a unique capability in this regard. However, full employment of these resources will not be enough.

The views of scientific experts receive wide acceptance when they are addressed to defining problems, but scientific opinion fares much less well when it proposes solutions to public problems. Articulating possible options for solution of these problems is more likely to be influential if it is done through intergovernmental international organizations (IOs), if they can effectively combine the capabilities of competent permanent secretariats with the political support and access to national expertise represented by member country delegations. Whatever their weaknesses, IOs have the crucial advantage that the full range of relevant (and sometimes irrelevant) public concerns and public values is represented in their debates. (These points are elaborated in Chapter 4.) Informing the affected publics and government officials in these matters will take time and collective effort. It is essential that due regard be given to the intrinsic differences among issues in regard to their potential impacts and their tractibility to effective political action.

A second essential ingredient for collective solutions is the availability of objective analyses of the potential social, economic, and environmental impacts of the technologies in question. While the first requirement is directed to the problem of public awareness and the creation of a climate of acceptance for collective action, the analyses called for here are directed at providing a base for official and expert efforts to structure workable solutions. In other words, the first is directed to "political will"; the second is directed to "political how." These analyses must be credible to responsible officials not only in terms of objectivity but also in terms of relevance and completeness. They are probably best undertaken by IOs, providing that national governments will accept their potential and authorize their acquisition of the necessary expert assistance.

Many of these problems, particularly those for which the adverse effects will accumulate gradually over a long time—for example, inadvertent modification of the stratosphere or possible leakage to the environment of the radioactive byproducts of nuclear power—pose special problems for collective action. Base line data need to be established (unfortunately, often after the base line has already been distorted by the effects in question). Rates of change, usually slow, must be determined through global deployment of sophisticated monitoring instruments. More difficult still, the level of publicly acceptable risk must be agreed on—a process dependent on slowly accumulating scientific evidence that characteristically involves controversy, dead ends, rejection of earlier interpretations, and apparent reversals in the thrust of expert opinion.[9] The state of science is not the only determinant, of course. Public perceptions of acceptable risk are in constant flux—a point amply demonstrated by such examples as automobile seat belts and the public response to warnings about the hazards of smoking—and it the relative assessment of hazard expressed in persuasive political terms that establishes the feasibility of political action for control.

Monitoring, base line studies, and assessments of relative risk are technological, not political, activities, and they are best undertaken by (politically credible) expert groups, such as ICSU, IIASA, or the specialized technical agencies of the UN.

When a common threat is credibly identified and articulated, and the political will for dealing with it through international collective action has ripened, a variety of options are, in principle, available. The choice among them depends not only on the nature of the issue but also on the dynamics of international politics at the time (see Chapter 9). The principal possibilities would seem to be (in order of effectiveness but also, obviously, of difficulty):

- National decisions, taken unilaterally or as a result of international concensus, to forgo the potential benefits of particular technological applications in light of the uncontrollability of their possible international repercussions.
- Binding international agreements.
- International monitoring of national actions, combined with enforcement powers.
- Creation of international control authorities with exclusive jurisdiction over the management of particular technologies.

Some of these possibilities are better adapted to particular problems than are others. History provides many examples of "binding" international agreements that failed to bind when put to the test. Most often, perhaps, this occurred because all the participants in the denouement were not signatories to the agreement or some who were had undergone major changes in government. Nonetheless, there are agreements in force in important areas that seem to be working, for example, the Antarctic Treaty of 1959 and the protocols that created INTELSAT.

The use of international monitoring combined with enforcement powers is exemplified, though incompletely, by the role of the International Atomic Energy Agency in the international safeguarding of nuclear materials. While IAEA's performance in this regard has come into question and undoubtedly needs strengthening, it is a mechanism in place, its structural shortcomings would appear to be correctible, and it is plausible that, given a sufficiency of political will in each of the adhering nations, IAEA could perform effectively in its assigned role. If this is true, and if developing events provide a convincing demonstration of its truth, the IAEA model might usefully be applied to other issues, such as the pollution of international waters.

In the face of the modestly optimistic assertions of the preceding paragraphs, it is only fair to point out that international organizations, with very limited exceptions, so far have not demonstrated the strengths attributed to them here. Chapter 9 offers some proposals for correcting this situation.

International *operational* control of the application of certain technologies that threaten national interests but lie beyond the reach of national authority poses an enormously more difficult challenge. Its achievement necessarily involves a deliberate surrender of a degree of national sovereignty that has no precedent in international affairs. Successful achievement of each of the ingredients of successful international collaborative action identified in the preceding paragraphs would be necessary, but not sufficient, preconditions. Binding and irrevocable commitment by each of the affected nations to accept the authority of a supranational control agency would be required—binding and irrevocable because unilateral denunciation of such an agreement would destroy its effectiveness without eliminating the problem. Practical sanctions against unilateral action are exceedingly difficult, if not impossible, to achieve. In addition to this basic and perhaps insurmountable difficulty, effective collective international operational control of a major technology would require the creation and continuous financial support of a body of expert international civil servants whose intellectual and emotional allegiance would be to global (or at least regional), as against national, interests and values. Some day this may all be possible, but it is clearly beyond the range of practicality at present and probably for a long time to come.

As an interim measure in dealing with issues like those identified above, and perhaps as an invaluable contribution to creating that climate of acceptance essential to effective international collective action, the international sharing of promising technologies—on appropriate terms, including appropriate safeguards—may be the best available strategy.

Notes

1. Dourmani, George A. *Exploiting the Resources of the Seabed*. Washington, D.C.: Congressional Research Service for the House Committee on Foreign Affairs, 1971. See also John A. Krauss, Marine Science and the 1974 Law of the Sea Conference. *Science*, 1974, **184,** 1335.

2. Chayes, Abram, Laskin, Paul, and Price, Monroe. *Direct Broadcasting from Satellites: Policies and Problems*. Washington, D.C.: The American Society of International Law, 1975.

3. Niblett, G.B.F. *Digital Information and the Privacy Problem*. OECD Information Series. Paris: Organisation for Economic Co-operation and Development, 1971.

4. *Inadvertant Climate Modification; A Study of Man's Impact on Climate*. Cambridge, Mass.: MIT Press, 1971.

5. UN Committee on the Peaceful Uses of Outer Space. *Review of National and International Space Activities for the Calendar Year 1975*. UN Document A/AC 105/167, February 20, 1976. See also the annual authorization hearings of the House Committee on Science and Technology and the Senate Committee on Aeronautics and Space Sciences, U.S. Congress.

6. For an analysis of the interaction between technological and political factors in the formulation of U.S. policy see Foreign Policy Issues Regarding Earth Resource Surveying by Satellite, A Report of the Secretary's Advisory Committee on Science and Foreign Affairs. Washington, D.C.: Department of State, July 1974. (unpublished document).

7. UN Committee on the Peaceful Uses of Outer Space. *Feasibility Study of a Possible Coordinating Function of the UN in Future Operational Activities in Remote Sensing from Satellites*. UN Document A/AC 105/154, January 9, 1976.

8. MacDonald, Gordon S. How to Wreck the Environment. In Nigel Calder (ed.), *Unless Peace Comes*. New York: Viking, 1968. It should be emphasized that Dr. MacDonald, an eminent environmentalist, was in no way endorsing such applications in his provocative paper.

9. The reader who would pursue this critical and difficult topic should start with William W. Lowrance, *Of Acceptable Risk: Science and the Determination of Safety*. Los Altos, Calif.: Kaufman, 1976.

9

NATIONAL AND
INTERNATIONAL
INSTITUTIONS

The bulk of the preceding chapters is devoted to an incomplete panorama of problems without obvious or appealing solutions. There is a clear need to balance this dismal recital with some answers or, at the least, possible approaches. The public policy issues raised here, and countless others like them, pose important and challenging intellectual problems: defining goals in operationally useful terms (and examining the total impacts that would accompany their achievement); analyzing alternative strategies; characterizing the optimum, the acceptable "fall-backs," and the wholly unacceptable among them; weighing the costs and benefits of different moves; probing previous work for methodological inadequacies and soft spots in assumptions and data; and so on. It is for other authors to explore these matters in detail. The focus here will be on institutional problems and how they might be dealt with. This approach may be something of a cop-out; I am fully aware of the widespread propensity within governments for proposing new organizational structures whenever the substantive issues seem to be intractable or the current solutions to them begin to look unpromising. Nevertheless, the most innovative ideas, the most careful analyses, and the greatest personal dedication get nowhere in governments (for very long, at least) without being institutionalized. Attention to structural and institutional problems is necessary, though it is never enough.

Before discussing institutional specifics, there are some general points that need to be made.

POLITICAL WILL

The first, and possibly most basic, point is that the successful conduct of foreign relations—to whatever ends we may individually and collectively direct this activity—requires something more than the good will of serious people traditionally invoked as the magic ingredient. It requires political will. Political will—the commitment of governments (more accurately, the national political leadership) to the pursuit of particular ends made in full recognition of the implied necessity to compromise other desirable ends—is not necessarily in conflict with good will (taken in the philosophical and moral sense), but it often appears to be. The United States, more than most other nations, has perceived its foreign relations in terms of higher principles and humanitarian ideals, and we usually act—when we do act—out of a conscious assumption of good will. When our actions are greeted with suspicion internationally and other governments denounce them as self-serving, misguided, and counterproductive, we are inclined to dismiss such criticisms as ill informed. We tend to see our political will, in foreign affairs at least, as a reflection of a basic good will and of policies that are the natural outgrowth of social principles that, in our view, are self-evidently successful. In Senator William Fulbright's phrase, we often exhibit the arrogance of power.

In the conduct of intergovernmental relations the presumption of mutual good will is a useful starting point, although not an essential precondition. Mutuality of self-interest is a more credible motivating force, in any event, though not as comforting to the sensibilities.

Political will is something else. It manifests itself one way or the other, by its exercise or by its absence, in every aspect of our national life. It is so common, and assumes so many disguises, that we don't always recognize it, but we know it's there and hope it can be counted on. Political will in the international arena is far less visible and far less comprehensible as a necessary ingredient of government. We can recognize it in our history in the various doctrines that have been laid down by presidents from Monroe to Nixon. We can recognize it, but that doesn't mean we understand it. In international relations political will is not often the product of the ballot box. Once we elect a President, who designates a Secretary of State, we are generally prepared to leave these largely remote and incomprehensible matters to the people we pay to deal with them. Though political will in international matters is usually a reflection of executive branch perceptions, intentions, and strategies, it is nonetheless dependent on the tacit, if not the active, support of the Congress. Indeed, on important occasions it has been the political will of the Congress that has prevailed over that of the executive to set our course. The tragic history of U.S. military involvement in Viet Nam is a perfect case in point.

INFORMING THE PUBLIC DEBATE

When political will is exercised by governments in areas that do not impinge directly or conspicuously on our ordinary lives—as is the case with most of the matters discussed in this volume—public understanding and acceptance are not easy to come by. At the same time, these international issues and many equally complex issues in other political, economic, and security areas do have important implications for our collective well-being. One conclusion must be that the policy-making process needs to be better illuminated for citizens and policy makers alike. This is easy to say but harder to accomplish. As a group, politicians have little interest in the substantive aspects of science and technology. By the same token, scientists and engineers have little interest in the substantive concerns of politics. (Presumably, this reflects the fact that more than pure chance segregated the individuals involved into their respective careers.) Ordinary Americans display little interest in either matter. Even when there is a serious desire to communicate, the various groups tend to talk past one another. C.P. Snow's "Two Cultures" concept is particularly relevant here, suitably modified to take account of the fact that there are more than two involved.

There are challenging questions with respect to how and by whom the policy debate on international technological matters is to be informed. The substance of the information required is not so difficult to define. There is no necessity to educate everyone in science and technology, economics, security problems, and international politics. What is needed is less comprehensive but more subtle. To contribute to public policy debate, each of us must know who does have the expertise to establish the facts central to the issues and to clarify their relevance. Equally, we must know when the experts have strayed beyond their area of expertise; in other words, we must be able to distinguish between objective knowledge and personal opinion, between relevance and red herrings. We need to know what is possible and what is not, technologically and politically.

We need these kinds of guidance in several contexts. We need credible *prospective analyses* about important problem areas that are evolving, informed anticipations of future events. Scientists are big on this, but unfortunately they have enjoyed a limited reception from politicians and the public at large (perhaps especially in those instances where they turned out to be right). There is clearly a problem of communications here that needs to be overcome. The difficulty may lie in scientists' professional habit of addressing their communications to their scientific peers. Certainly, the communications problem is complicated by the fact that scientific perceptions address the longer term, while political concerns focus on the immediate. It wouldn't make sense to try to change that; the world needs both. What might make sense is to try to develop in the technological area institutional capabilities and commitments counterpart to the recently emerging (and on the whole immensely valuable) legal groups concentrating on public interest matters. A Ralph Nader for international technology could be a valuable asset.

The technology community, the politicians, and all the rest of us need a clearer explication of the available *policy alternatives* for dealing with these issues, including a credibly objective assessment of the costs, risks, and benefits that accompany each. We need to understand better how the various policy alternatives for dealing with one kind of issues interact with established policies in other important areas; how various policy alternatives for conserving energy would interact with existing environmental policies, taxation policies, and labor policies, for example. This important activity, which might be called policy analysis, is being undertaken, in a preliminary way at least, by a variety of university and nonprofit research organizations, by the National Academies of Science and Engineering, and by the recently established Office of Technology Assessment of the Congress, among others. The effort needs to be broadened and its conceptual and methodological underpinnings strengthened.

The policy-making process needs *retrospective analysis*, also. It is important to understand rationally (and not mythologically, anecdotally, or ideologically, as is so often the case) why some public policy measures accomplished their intended purposes while others did not (or incurred unintended disbenefits in other areas). Only in this way can the policy-making process expect to improve. University libraries have shelves full of material on such topics, but these have had little impact on actual policy making. A more effective approach may be to make fuller use of the investigative capabilities of relevant Congressional committees. Well-planned and appropriately documented public hearings can make a very great positive contribution to the development of policy on a wide range of important public issues.

The remainder of this chapter deals with the domestic and international institutionalization of political mechanisms for dealing with technology-related issues. These structures have both valuable strengths and formidable weaknesses. It is important to understand them and their interactions, because these are the current embodiments of the mechanisms by which our collective interests and aspirations will be achieved, if they are achieved at all.

DOMESTIC INSTITUTIONAL ARRANGEMENTS

The various international technology issues discussed in the earlier chapters of this book clearly demonstrate the need for institutional structures within the U.S. government to:

- Provide technically competent and politically informed analysis of important technical and economic issues.
- Develop policy options and strategies for implementing them.
- Provide objective evaluations of the feasibility, costs, benefits, and potential side effects of major technological programs proposed for government support.
- Examine the consequences of foreign government policies for U.S. agency R&D programs, for the international competitiveness of U.S. industry, and for other priority national interests.
- Assist the federal R&D and regulatory agencies in interpreting established policies and applying them equitably and effectively.
- Insure coordinated representation of U.S. interests in international negotiations relating to technology policy and in the multilateral programs of international organizations whose activities impinge importantly on U.S. interests.

As technology is a pervasive factor in the whole panoply of federal government activities, so the needs for adequate and relevant staff competence in technology and for its effective organization extend across all the branches of government: Legislative, Executive, and Judicial. (It is increasingly important at the state and municipal levels, also, but that problem is beyond the scope of this book.)

The Congress has shown an increasing sensitivity to this need in increased attention to:

- Recruiting professionally competent scientists and engineers to the staffs of House and Senate committees operating in this area.
- Increasing demands for competent analysis of technology-related issues by such supporting agencies as the Congressional Research Service and the General Accounting Office.
- Creation of ad hoc specialist bodies such as the Commission on Government Procurement.
- Establishment of the Office of Technology Assessment.

Much has been accomplished, including, in addition to those examples cited, the recent reorganization of the committee structure of the Congress into a more rational mechanism for dealing with these and other equally important broad public interests. But ample room for continued improvement remains.

The situation in the federal courts (and in the hearing tribunals of the various federal regulatory agencies, where a comparable problem exists) is not as sanguine as that in the Congress. Increasingly, important and precedent-setting cases (for example, those dealing with the role of environmental impact statements) involve technological issues, but the access of the judiciary to technically competent expert advice serving in a pro bono publico capacity is very limited; no viable mechanism has been identified—let alone put into place—to identify specific needs and appropriate ways to meet them. The problem is increasingly conspicuous in respect to domestic issues; although less visible, it is crucial to international legal concerns as well, as exemplified by patent matters, restrictive business practices legislation, law-of-the-sea issues, environmental control problems, and so on.

The executive branch remains that element of the U.S. government most pervasively involved in technology policy issues. This involvement occurs at several levels, and it is helpful to look at these separately.

The federal technical agencies and those cabinet-level departments with substantial R&D activities each have significant interests in international arrangements important to the fulfillment of their domestic missions; virtually without exception they have created staff structures with specific responsibilities in this area. Some of them—particularly those such as NASA and the Department of Energy, whose enabling legislation makes specific reference to the international dimensions of their responsibilities—have become powerful and virtually independent spokesmen for U.S. foreign policy in their particular areas. The Department of Defense is a case in point. Its cooperative R&D relationships with NATO and its central role in cooperative arrangements with foreign allies for offshore production of U.S.–originated weapons systems, to say nothing of the sheer size of its technological operations, have given it a major and largely independent role in important aspects of U.S. international technological policy. It is true that the National Security Council provides general policy guidance in these matters, and that the Bureau of Politico-Military Affairs of the Department of State and the Arms Control and Disarmament Agency (an otherwise independent agency reporting to the Secretary of State) provide a degree of review, and sometimes leavening, of Defense policies and international technology programs. However, Defense's powerful Congressional constituency and its two voices in most interagency policy analysis exercises (the Secretary of Defense and the Chairman of the Joint Chiefs of Staff are customarily represented by separate participants) give it a preeminent role.

In addition to the technical agencies themselves, there are other cabinet-level departments and Executive Office entities whose charters give them a major role in determining and implementing U.S. technological policy: the Departments of Commerce, Agriculture, Treasury, Justice, and of course, State; the National Security Council (NSC); the Office of Science and Technology Policy (OSTP); the Council on International Economic Policy (CIEP); the Office of Telecommunications Policy (OTP); and the Domestic Council (whose concerns and decisions in technology-related matters usually have important international implications) have been the most conspicuous. The Office of Management and Budget, speaking with a powerful voice in setting priorities and coordinating executive branch positions on legislative proposals, has an obvious, if less direct, role. So do a dozen other executive branch entities, each with special concerns but all impinging on international technology matters. None of these departments, councils, and the like are equipped with a breadth and depth of staff technological competence commensurate with their responsibilities and decision-making authority in these matters. For the most part, their principals, whether political appointees or career officials, are not aware of any special need in this area, preferring to rely on the technological expertise of other elements of the executive branch, including some who have a vested interest in the outcome.

The problems implicit in the work of these arms of the executive branch go beyond those already raised in Chapter 2 with respect to independent technological expertise. Each of these entities is importantly concerned with establishing national objectives, strategies, and priorities, matters that often cannot be intelligently addressed without informed consideration of technological constraints and technological opportunities. Each of them is engaged, from time to time at least, in representing the U.S. government in bilateral and multilateral international discussions and negotiations regarding issues in which technology plays a major role. Some statistics demonstrate the importance of this involvement:[1] In 1974, forty-five agencies of government *other than the Department of State* provided 56 percent of the official U.S. representation to international conferences—a total of more than 2,000 delegates. In the same year, of nearly 10,000 civilian bureaucrats stationed in overseas embassies and consulates, more than 20 percent were employees of agencies other than State. It is a continuing challenge to the executive branch, and one responded to inadequately, to insure that the positions and the political tactics espoused by U.S. delegates to these meetings are thoughtfully considered, informed, and coordinated in regards to their technological implications, and take into proper account the totality of U.S. interests rather than focusing narrowly on the mission-related interests of specific federal agencies.

The National Security Council has played a vital role in this respect.* In important policy matters that require specialist expertise for their analysis, including most technology-related matters, NSC customarily employed interagency working groups to define the issues, set out the relevant background, identify feasible policy responses, and set forth for decision makers the objective arguments for and against particular possibilities. Considering the complexity of the issues and the strongly held views characteristic of the participating agencies in almost any issue of importance, this system has

---

* On taking office President Carter announced his intention to substantially reduce the staff of the NSC and to abolish the CIEP. Hopefully, those important coordinating functions described here will continue to be performed with equal effectiveness at some point proximate to the President.

worked reasonably well. The reasons for its success (when it succeeded) include, certainly:

- The timeliness and importance of the specific issues considered.
- The judgment and skill of NSC staffers in formulating the charge
  to the working group and insuring that the group effort remained
  reasonably within the bounds set.
- The willingness and ability of the individual working group participants to set aside agency positions while they formulated the
  relevant background considerations and identified feasible alternative responses. This was made possible by two unstated but
  essential ground rules for the conduct of these exercises: First, the
  language in which the pros and cons of possible policy alternatives was stated was left to the adherents of the respective positions and didn't require concensus of the whole group. Second,
  agency recommendations on the choice of policy options were
  sought *after* the text of the study memorandum was agreed, thus
  affording a separate opportunity for the participants to espouse
  their respective convictions and indulge their passions within
  their agency environments.

It must be admitted, however, that the NSC's successes were
often limited in scope and utility, dealing with highly specific issues
rather than developing broader guidelines that, had they been available, might have obviated the need to deal with the specifics at the
NSC level. On the other hand, it is dealing successfully with
specifics that is the end game and the ultimate test of the utility of
guidelines. A greater balance between the two kinds of efforts
would seem a worthwhile goal, even if it proves impossible to
achieve.

The State Department

It would seem obvious that the Department of State should play a
central role in the development and implementation of U.S. government policy in international issues relating to technology. State's
traditional role in foreign policy matters, the breadth and depth of
its bureaucratic involvement in foreign relations, and perhaps most
important, its special relationship to U.S. ambassadors and embas-

sies overseas would seem to dictate a preeminent role. In fact, while State is heavily and unavoidably involved, its authority and responsibility in such affairs is at best ambiguous, and is often challenged or ignored by other elements of government (and sometimes of the private sector as well). Whether a cause or an effect of this situation, the standing of international technology policy issues and of those individual members and institutional elements of the federal bureaucracy particularly concerned with them has never been high in the Department of State, and sometimes dips below the level of visibility.[2] Paradoxically, one of the most important reasons for this situation is the pervasiveness of technological dimensions in foreign affairs. To understand how this comes about, it is necessary to understand something of the organization of the State Department and the traditions of the Foreign Service.

State is organized, as are many large bureaucracies including large industrial enterprises, in a two-dimensional structure. Put another way, the Department of State is structured like a crossword puzzle, in which the operative words must fit both horizontal and vertical constraints; the unavoidable result is a degree of ambiguity in definition and a large number of "black holes." Line authority for the conduct of foreign relations extends from the President through the Secretary of State and his deputy through assistant secretaries who head regional bureaus to the ambassadors overseas (who are legally personal representatives of the President). The regional bureaus—European, African, Far East, and the like—collectively cover the whole globe and are each responsible for every aspect of foreign relations within their prescribed geographic areas. Cutting across this structure are functional or staff bureaus, also headed (in most cases) by assistant secretaries: Economic and Business Affairs, Politico-Military Affairs, and so on. Within this functional structure there is a Bureau of Oceans and International Environmental and Scientific Affairs (OES).

Principal responsibility for overall coordination and management rests with undersecretaries for Economic Affairs; Security Assistance, Science and Technology; and Political Affairs (the concerns of the last being focused on the regional bureaus). These, together with a legal advisor and various planning and administrative elements, are expected to assist the Secretary of State in keeping the gears of this complex machinery properly meshed and lubricated and, hopefully, turning at a reasonable speed. (This metaphor should not be examined too closely by those readers familiar with the principles of mechanics, who would undoubtedly perceive that it ignores the possibility of "idler gears" that reverse the direction of movement

—a concept not entertained, so far as is known, by those responsible for the machinery of government.)

This fascinating organism is further complicated by the existence of otherwise independent agencies concerned with basic aspects of foreign relations but integrated with State only by the fact that their principal officers report to the Secretary of State. The most important of these, in terms of the interests of this volume, are the Agency for International Development (responsible for technical assistance to the less developed countries) and the Arms Control and Disarmament Agency (ACDA), responsible, among other things, for assessment of the technological feasibility of international arms control measures and the means for verifying them.

There is considerable overlapping of interest and ambiguity of responsibility throughout. (Even the particular jurisdictions of the undersecretaries are not always clear.) These complications and the manifold interests of the State Department weaken its potential as an effective focus for government-wide policy formulation in international technology issues. In general, those technology policy issues for which State's leadership regards the *political* dimension as preeminent are customarily assigned to the regional bureaus. Those seen as primarily *military* in character (which includes most nuclear issues) are assigned to Politico-Military Affairs or to ACDA. Issues seen as basically *economic,* such as assuring energy supplies, are given to the Bureau of Economic and Business Affairs. *Technical assistance* matters go to AID. The responsibility for S&T relations with *UN organizations* is largely the responsibility of the Bureau of International Organization Affairs, which is short of the resources necessary to an adequate substantive effort.

Since 1951 State has had an office or bureau specifically mandated with the principal departmental responsibility for scientific and technological affairs. Writing in 1967, Eugene Skolnikoff, who had observed State's struggles in the S&T arena from the vantage point of the White House science advisory apparatus, described its history and analyzed its inadequacies.[3] His absorbing chronicle led him to conclusions that remain largely valid today. Skolnikoff points out that while the responsibilities of the succession of institutional mechanisms employed by the State Department over the years always provided that the science element should "participate broadly in general foreign policy development, ensuring that appropriate consideration is given to scientific and technological factors," and designated it as "the point of coordination" between State and the technical agencies, the actual scope of activity and influence was quite narrowly circumscribed.

In its earlier years State's science office was primarily concerned with international activities facilitating the U.S. scientific community in its relationships with its overseas peers. Technology issues, when visualized at all, were seen as the concerns of other elements of the department or of other federal agencies. A strong element of this bias still remains. The strength and persistence of this conception of State's role can be quite justifiably regarded as reflecting both the resident scientists' perceptions of foreign policy and of the Department leadership's perceptions of science and technology. It is strongly reinforced, as suggested earlier, by the traditions and professional conceptions of the Foreign Service. The Foreign Service—separate from but counterpart to the Civil Service—is characterized by long-standing traditions, strongly reinforced by its personnel placement policies and practices, that emphasize the generalist rather than the specialist as the ideal. Officers specializing in science and engineering are generally placed in the reserve officer category with limited term appointments. Careers in technology-related matters are virtually nonexistent.

From time to time the Congress has expressed interest in a broader policy role for State in international S&T policy matters. In 1973, legislation was adopted that directed the Secretary of State to create a Bureau of Oceans and International Environmental and Scientific Affairs (OES), to be headed by an assistant secretary. The legislation initially introduced, which came from two Senatorial sources with quite different interests, would have created two bureaus—one for fisheries matters and another for environmental matters. Neither had the support of the department's leadership. The compromise reached was to combine the two proposals and add science, which was not a consideration in the original offerings. In implementing this legislation the department defined the scope of the new bureau's concerns to include:[4] "functions relating to international scientific, technological, environmental, weather, oceans, atmosphere, fisheries, wildlife, conservation, health, population, and related matters." The implementing document goes on to say that "the Bureau's responsibility for technological matters will include atomic energy and energy-related research and development, space technology, and other advanced technological developments except those which are primarily defense related." In describing OES' functions, the department gives it "primary responsibility for the development of comprehensive and coherent U.S. policies in the areas where it has been assigned functional responsibility." Although this broad charge had its genesis in the Congressional legislation, the actual authority it confers depends, of course, on the willingness of the technical agencies and the elements of the White House staff involved (all of whom have charters that overlap into this area) to accept its exercise. The attitude of the Secretary of State toward these matters and his willingness to exert his authority on behalf of his own bureau's policy recommendations is crucial.

OES does play a role in technology policy issues (as did the predecessor bureau), but often as a participant in interagency working groups organized under the aegis of the National Security Council or other White House entities. Considering the limitations on its staff resources (only a handful have advanced training and experience in technology) and the general lack of interest in technology matters that has been characteristic of State's leadership in the past, it is unlikely that OES—or any other organizational element of the State Department—can ever play a true leadership role in international technology-related policy making.

EXECUTIVE BRANCH FOCUS

If no single department can play an effective leadership role in developing policies regarding international technology matters, who can? As implied above, those departments that possess the effective authority needed for leadership in an area where agency perspectives (and even objectives) are often in apparent conflict generally are not seized with technology policy issues as a priority concern and do not have the expert staff necessary to deal with them. Specialized technical agencies, on the other hand, do not have the charter or the political "clout" to deal with the issues in any comprehensive fashion.

Prior to the dissolution of the Office of Science and Technology and the President's Science Advisory Committee in 1973, OST, under the direction of a series of President's Science Advisors, was the major impetus behind interagency efforts to deal with international technology policy matters and was able to exercise considerable influence in resolving major differences in agency positions. This was possible not only because of the aura of authority that proximity to the President cast over the Science Advisor and his staff, but also because of the relatively close relationships that had evolved between OST and the Office of Management and Budget, the National Security Council, and, in the later period of its existence, the Council on International Economic Policy and the Domestic Council (many of whose activities and interests impinged on international technological issues). The Federal Council for Science and Technology (FCST), traditionally chaired by the Science Advisor, provided a mechanism under the effective control of OST for inter-agency consideration of policy matters cutting across the interests of the various technical agencies. Skillful orchestration of these inter-locking relationships by the various Science Advisors produced a body of analyses, evaluations, and policy options that did much to shape U.S. policies on international technology matters from the late 1950s until 1973.

President Nixon's Reorganization Plan of 1973 abolished OST, the President's Science Advisory Committee, and the Space and Aeronautics Council, and designated by name the Director of the National Science Foundation (NSF) as Science Advisor. The new plan gave the responsibility for S&T advice relating to national security matters to the NSC, but left standing the Federal Council for Science and Technology, designating the new Science Advisor as its chairman. A Science and Technology Policy Office was created within, but essentially separate from, the NSF to support the new arrangement; and its staff—several of them drawn from the old OST—set out to recapture as much as possible of the earlier respon-sibilities, relationships, and momentum of OST. The S&T commu-nity, within and outside the government, understandably regarded the Reorganization Plan as a vote of no confidence in the need for and activities of the White House S&T policy apparatus, however, and the new arrangements never achieved the recognition accorded to the earlier setup. Almost immediately, the S&T community re-sponded with proposals for reestablishment of an S&T apparatus within the White House.

In June 1975 President Ford offered legislation to the Congress that, in effect, recreated the science and technology advisory ap-paratus in the White House. As finally enacted nearly a year later, the legislation restored, with few changes, all the elements and pre-rogatives of the earlier structure, with the exception of the Presi-dent's Science Advisory Committee. (Both the executive and legisla-tive branches have become wary of institutionalizing sources for possibly unpalatable advice.) The legislation (Public Law 94–282) adds a new element—a statement of U.S. S&T policy that includes the following principles:

- "The continuing development and implementation of strategies . . . based upon a continuous appraisal of the role of S&T in achieving goals and formulating policies of the U.S. . . . ."
- "The establishment of S&T to foster a healthy economy . . . com-patible with prudent and frugal use of resources and with the preservation of a benign environment."

- "The conduct of S&T . . . to serve domestic needs while promoting policy objectives."
- "Maintenance of a solid base for S&T in the U.S. . . ."

There is nothing startling here, but enactment as public law some things that the Congress, public officials, and individual scientists and engineers have said for years is comforting. (The ideas left out might tell us something, too.)

The international dimension is, for reasons argued elsewhere in this book, inseparably related to domestic policy and its objectives. It should, therefore, constitute a principal area of concern of the Federal technology policy apparatus, however that is institutionalized. Every element of domestic technology policy has international implications and must operate in an environment in which international influences play a major role. Whatever means are employed to deal with such matters as government patent policy, R&D procurement policy, product standards, and countless other technology policy concerns must be considered in an international context. The realities of geopolitics impose their own requirements for technology policy responses—requirements independent of, and sometimes in conflict with, domestic interests and priorities. The technology policy-making apparatus must deal effectively with this dimension as well. Technology is a means, not an end in itself, so that the development of technology policy by the federal government must serve the interests of, and be consistent with the strategies and priorities established by, other aspects of government. In the international arena, as has been suggested earlier, this requires a close and mutually respectful relationship between the federal technology policy apparatus and OMB, NSC, CIEP, and the Domestic Council (or those successor organizations that may emerge), as well as with numerous elements of the cabinet-level departments and, of course, the technical agencies.

INTERNATIONAL INSTITUTIONAL STRUCTURES

There are a variety of international structures that deal in one way or another with technological questions. Many of these are non-governmental in composition, though some of the most important of those are funded in large part by governmental subventions. A conspicuous and important example is the International Council of Scientific Unions (ICSU). It is composed of seventeen autonomous international scientific unions (in such areas as astronomy, pure and applied chemistry, and radio sciences) and more than sixty national members (academies of science, research councils, or similar scientific institutions). A primary function is the planning and coordination of major international scientific programs, such as the International Geophysical Year (IGY), many of which involve cooperation with international intergovernmental organizations, such as the World Meteorological Organization, as well as with the constituent national nongovernmental members.

In addition to such quasi-governmental international organizations as ICSU, there are international professional scientific and engineering societies as well as those concerned with managerial and political aspects of technology (e.g., the Atlantic Council). Each of these nongovernmental international organizations has interests in areas that overlap the topics dealt with in earlier chapters, but the focus for the remainder of this chapter is on multilateral governmental organizations (IOs).

International intergovernmental institutional structures created to deal with technological issues are by no means new. For example, in 1865 twenty European nations formed the International Telegraph Union, whose jurisdiction was expanded two decades later to include international telephone services. The International Radiotelegraph Union was created in 1900 to insure the rational development of radio communications; the United States became a participant in 1912. The two organizations merged, in 1932, to form the International Telecommunications Union (ITU), which became a specialized agency of the United Nations after World War II.

The proliferation of IOs specializing in technological matters, or dealing with broader issues driven or constrained by technology, has become enormous. In 1975 the United States participated (usually providing funding proportionate to its GNP) in more than twenty such IOs, and an uncountable number of committees, councils, expert groups, and working parties organized within this structure. In addition, the United States officially participated in 817 intergovernmental conferences in 1975, a majority of them concerned with technological matters.[5]

Some IOs, such as the ITU, are specifically devoted to technological matters. Another group, including, for example, the (UN) Food and Agriculture Organization and the World Meteorological Organization, is concerned with operations involving the applications of technology. Still others, such as the OECD, UNESCO, and the UN Environmental Program (UNEP), are heavily focused on matters of technology policy. The fastest growing group, and in geopolitical

terms the most important, are those IOs that are primarily con-
cerned with technology as a factor in socioeconomic development:
the UN Conference on Trade and Development (UNCTAD), the UN
Development Program (UNDP), the Organization of American
States (OAS), the Consultative Group on International Agricultural
Research (CGIAR), and so on.

National membership in international organizations is, of course,
voluntary. Admission to membership requires the approval of a
majority of the member states, and membership incurs the obliga-
tion to contribute financial support (usually in proportion to GNP).
Failure to pay these assessments—a common occurrence—means
forfeiture of voting rights but not the right to be represented and
to participate in the debate. Since so much bloc voting occurs and
balloting outcomes are seldom close, it is the debate that largely matters.

Most IOs conduct their formal business on a one nation–one vote
basis, though some employ weighted voting and others act by consensus. All of them have permanent secretariats. By their ability to
determine agenda and prepare the working papers on which the
debate is centered, the secretariats frequently wield considerable
authority.

IOs perform a variety of tasks that are vital to international relations. These have been ranked by Joseph Nye in "ascending order of
difficulty" as follows: (1) provision of information, (2) formulation of
general norms, (3) regulation and monitoring of state behavior in accordance with specific norms, and (4) operation of technologies or
elaborate monitoring and planning systems.[6] The capabilities Nye
has listed have important implications. With respect to the information function, for example, IOs can sometimes gain access to national data not otherwise available to other nations (at least in a form
comparable with domestic data) and disseminate comparative data
to very wide audiences. Frequently the creation of information functions in IOs has led national governments to establish their own information and statistical capabilities where none existed previously.
The information function has another subtly important function as
well. By forcing agreement on definitions of statistical parameters,
and on those parameters that are to be compared, it helps to defuse
the rhetoric that often accompanies statistics when these are used as
surrogates for politically important goals.

"Formulation of general norms" reflects the importance of open
debate and global exposure in gaining adherence to principles and
positions that national governments might otherwise be reluctant to
accept. IOs have a further advantage in this regard. Being freed from

the direct constraints of domestic politics, and especially from the priority-forcing impact of domestic electoral cycles, IOs can consider important issues that are not (and perhaps cannot be) given adequate priority in the national political process. IOs can undertake long-term activities and can consider options for longer term political action that would otherwise not be seriously debated in the national context.

Nye also points out that perhaps the most important function of IOs is the way they affect agenda setting in world politics. The massive UN conferences on the environment, food, population, water, and the like, with the attention and interest they create in the media and the world scientific and technological communities, have enormous impact on national as well as international political agendas. Obviously, different IOs will approach a particular issue in different ways; a debate on technology in trade may come out quite differently in UNCTAD than in GATT (General Agreement on Tariffs and Trade). The choice of forum, then, becomes a major consideration in the conduct of multilateral politics. As Nye remarks, "Government officials shop among forums as they try to steer issues to arenas more favorable to their preferred outcomes; and they use international organizations to bring pressure on other governments as well as other departments of their own governments." The last point is particularly evident in interagency debates about S&T priorities. The findings and recommendations of international conferences provide an "aura of legitimacy" for agency programs in the competition for leadership roles and for funds.

The actual accomplishment of these roles by IOs, even in "nonpolitical" areas, is surrounded with difficulties. Staff resources are inadequate (in scope and appropriate expertise), national member priorities differ, asymmetries among national institutional capabilities make participation in common efforts and even meaningful communications among participants very difficult, private sector interests (especially those of MNCs) may appear threatened at the same time that expertise found largely in the private sector may be essential to success, and even the most promising mid- and longer term programs may be sacrificed to new crisis efforts.

A typical history illustrating each of these difficulties is represented by the efforts of the World Health Organization (WHO) to develop effective responses to the pressures from nearly all of its members for the international regulation of pharmaceutical drugs.[7] The post–World War II period has brought enormous advances in pharmacology and corresponding increases in world trade in ethical drugs. By the early 1950s the major drug-producing nations had created a variety of legal and regulatory control mechanisms to insure the quality, efficacy, and safety of the pharmaceuticals in domestic commerce, but few extended those controls to drugs produced for export. Furthermore, since some of these control measures had the effect of nontariff barriers to trade, the major manufacturers rapidly became multinational, producing locally in each of their major markets. The LDCs, on the other hand, lacking both technically strong indigenous producers and effective national control systems, felt they were endangered by imports of generally unfamiliar drugs of uncertain quality and efficacy, often at high prices. As early as 1951, under LDC pressure the WHO called for a meeting of national regulatory authorities "to consider the advantages of more uniform methods for the control of [ethical] drugs in the various countries in the interests of health and international commerce."[8] The WHO has been increasingly involved ever since, but its record of achievement is disappointing.

The WHO tried a variety of approaches as members' perceptions of the priority issues evolved. It is beyond the scope of this book to detail this history here,[9] but it is useful for our broader purposes to outline briefly the major tasks addressed, the corresponding modalities adopted, and the apparent reasons for lack of success.

The initial concern, as indicated earlier, was with the effect of national regulations as a nontariff barrier to trade. This issue was rendered moot by rapid multinationalization of the industry. In the early 1960s international concern had shifted to the dangers posed by drugs of low quality moving in international commerce. The LDCs pressed insistently on WHO for international action; between 1963 and 1974 no less than seventeen resolutions addressed specifically to this issue were adopted.

As is so often the case in similar circumstances, action was demanded in the virtually total absence of specific data or even of the monitoring capabilities required to develop it. The WHO successively attempted five different programs:

- The creation of regional testing facilities. This idea ran afoul of budgetary problems, the inability of the LDC clients to agree on regional groupings and locations for the planned facilities, and the general lack of cooperation from the drug manufacturers (who understandably denied the existence of a problem).
- Assistance in the training and upgrading of national regulatory capabilities through regional seminars. This effort, very inadequately funded, continued for a decade without ever achieving operational viability.

- Attempts to formulate principles defining "good manufacturing practice." (U.S. quality control procedures, for instance, do not generally rely on batch inspection, but rather on detailed regulations governing good manufacturing practice.) The recommendations of a group of experts were adopted without serious debate, probably because they were nonbinding and very general and, in some respects, ambiguous.

- National certification of the quality of exported pharmaceuticals. This plan floundered for two reasons: four of the major exporters' exempting production for export from national regulatory requirements, and possible deterioration of quality in shipment and storage under often adverse conditions of temperature and humidity.

- Monitoring of adverse reactions to drugs.

The last-named program took on special priority only recently, largely as a result of the thalidomide disaster in 1961–1962, and has been the major focus of recent U.S. initiatives in the WHO. A major pilot project was initiated in 1968, entirely funded by the United States, with twelve nations participating. The results were sufficiently encouraging so that WHO assumed funding responsibility in 1971 and, by the end of 1974, twenty countries were participating. By 1976, however, WHO funding had been emasculated, and the project may not survive.

The basic reasons for apparent failure of what appeared to be a flourishing and valuable joint international undertaking were two. The first appears to be generic to such efforts in any field, no matter how humanitarian the purpose. The LDCs came to see the program as having little relevance to their pressing health needs, and wanted to free the funding for other, newer programs. The second, though unique to the adverse reaction reporting system, may shed light on another reason for the lack of interest among the LDCs. Adverse drug reactions can be observed only at the clinical level—not at the laboratory or in the manufacturing process—so the reports on which the system is based must be filed by individual doctors and nurses. Not only does this create major administrative problems, particularly in an LDC, but major sociological and psychological problems as well. Many physicians argue that without a great deal of detailed background on the patient, the illness treated, and other drugs employed, adverse reaction reports are useless at best and may be misleading. Furthermore, filing such reports is often viewed by patients (or their survivors) as tantamount to admission of malpractice. Sic transit a glorious scheme.

WEAKNESSES OF INTERNATIONAL ORGANIZATIONS

The capabilities and political influence of IOs are accompanied by serious weaknesses. The most obvious of these, and perhaps the most important, is the one nation–one vote principle, the provision that, for example, gives a citizen of Gabon 1,000 times the voting power in the UN General Assembly as a citizen of India. The voting problem is greatly exacerbated by the practice of bloc voting and the increasing tendency to employ bloc voting power to inject unrelated politicalization into technical debates, as in the condemnations of Israel injected into discussions by the Arab-led bloc ranging from world housing needs to the conduct of research in archaeology. In recent years the debate on technical assistance to the less developed countries has been dominated by the bloc voting strength of the LDCs, under the leadership of Brazil, Algeria, the Philippines, and others. In this debate the LDCs have undertaken a major effort to coalesce views and develop agreed proposals through bilateral consultations and carefully planned regional meetings. U.S. officials responsible in these matters have been less than alert to the importance of these activities and sometimes slow to grasp the extent to which the LDC bloc is influencing the positions of other technologically advanced countries.

The utility of IOs as forums for informed debate and the evolution of useful programs and effective policies has been greatly handicapped by the manner in which national representatives to IOs are chosen by most countries and the inadequacies of the backup these representatives receive in national capitals. Sophisticated technological issues are frequently debated by politicians and foreign ministry officials who have no expertise regarding them nor any support of knowlegeable bureaucrats and private sector representatives either at the meeting or in their national capitals. This situation, bad as it is, is worsened by the existence of so many different international forums dealing with the same or overlapping issues. Even now the U.S. government has no formal mechanism for soliciting interagency views or those of affected groups in the private sector on a host of important issues being debated in various IOs, or for insuring consistency among the positions taken by the U.S. delegates to different forums.

Another persistent problem of IOs is the composition of their permanent secretariats, the credibility of the expertise they bring to issues in debate, and their basic objectivity. The secretariats of IOs are generally designated by the respective secretaries general, but the selection process is not at all free from political influence.

Behind-the-scenes jockeying by permanent national delegations and voting blocs is a major, and usually determining, influence on the choice of individuals (and their national origins) for important secretariat positions. While the level of competence is generally high, objectivity is often sorely missing. This circumstance greatly weakens the effectiveness of the relationships between permanent secretariats and the international political bodies they are created to serve.

A final weakness of IOs that requires particular mention is their inability to enforce compliance with their decisions, or even to determine (without the cooperation of the government involved) whether an agreed norm is being observed. The problem is perhaps unsolvable. In the end, any nation can unilaterally renounce its membership in any international organization. Any nation that does so, of course, risks incurring penalties that can be severe: trade sanctions, the closing of international borders to movement of its citizens, suspension of international communications of all kinds. However, history has not provided convincing demonstrations of the efficacy of these measures. The most populous of the world's nations existed, quite successfully, entirely outside any formal international framework for a quarter of a century. While the United States went to war in Korea in the name of its obligations to the UN, there are few other such instances, and it is doubtful that this will happen again.[10]

For all of their weaknesses, IOs must be taken seriously, and efforts to increase their effectiveness must receive priority attention. If the preceding chapters in this book have accomplished at all my purpose, they have demonstrated that the press of advancing technology demands that the community of nations develop effective means to channel the directions of technological application, to achieve reasonable equity in allocating its benefits and costs, and to insure that the impacts of technology always remain within the reach of collective political authority and will. The age of hegemony is behind us. Only collective multilateral action can extend the reach of public policy to the ever-expanding grasp of technology. International organizations—credible, effective, dependable—are essential to collective global action.

To achieve more effective IOs we must inform and motivate not only the government officials and secretariats involved, but all aspects of government and of the body politic. You and I must accept a responsibility to recognize, to understand, to articulate, viable options and the essential need to balance risks and benefits, and to find acceptable compromises among the needs and aspirations of people everywhere. We all must.

Notes

1. Nye, Joseph S., Jr. Independence and Interdependence. *Foreign Policy,* Spring 1976, 138–139.
2. Huddle, Franklin P. *Science and Technology in the Department of State: Bringing Technical Content Into Diplomatic Policy and Operations.* Washington, D.C.: Congressional Research Service for the House Committee on International Relations, 1975. See also T. Keith Glennan, *Technology and Foreign Affairs.* Washington, D.C.: Department of State, 1976.
3. Skolnikoff, Eugene B. *Science, Technology and American Foreign Policy.* Cambridge, Mass.: MIT Press, 1967.
4. Foreign Affairs Manual Circular 687. Washington, D.C.: Department of State, 1974.
5. Nye, Independence and Interdependence.
6. Nye, Independence and Interdependence. This topic is also examined in greater detail in Eugene B. Skolnikoff, *The International Imperatives of Technology: Technological Development and the International Political System.* Berkeley, Calif.: Institute of International Studies, University of California, 1972.
7. Kay, David A. *The International Regulation of Pharmaceutical Drugs.* Washington, D.C.: American Society of International Law, 1975.
8. World Health Organization, Document No. EB7R79, 1951.
9. See Kay, *International Regulation.*
10. Russett, Bruce. *Power and Community in World Politics.* San Francisco: W.H. Freeman, 1974. Chapter 19 (with John D. Sullivan) attacks the IO enforcement concept in an analysis based on the economists' theories of "collective goods."

LIST OF ACRONYMS

ABM	Anti-Ballistic Missile
ACAST	Advisory Committee for the Application of Science and Technology to Development (UN)
ACDA	Arms Control and Disarmament Agency (U.S.)
AEC	Atomic Energy Commission (U.S.)
AID	Agency for International Development (U.S.)
APS	American Physical Society
CGIAR	Consultative Group on International Agricultural Research
CIEP	Council on International Economic Policy (U.S.)
DOD	Department of Defense (U.S.)
EC	European Community (sometimes European Economic Community)
ECOSOC	Economic and Social Council (UN)
ERDA	Energy Research and Development Administration (U.S.)
EURODIF	Consortium for uranium enrichment by the diffusion process (France, Belgium, Italy, and Spain)
FAO	Food and Agriculture Organization (UN)
FCST	Federal Council for Science and Technology (U.S.)
GATT	General Agreement on Tariffs and Trade
GNP	Gross national product

IAEA	International Atomic Energy Agency (UN)
ICSU	International Council of Scientific Unions
IEA	International Energy Agency
IEP	International Environmental Program (UN)
IGY	International Geophysical Year
IIASA	International Institute for Applied Systems Analysis
INFCEP	International Nuclear Fuel Cycle Evaluation Program
INTELSAT	International Telecommunications Satellite program
IO	International (intergovernmental) organization
ITU	International Telecommunications Union (UN)
KIST	Korean Institute for Science and Technology
LACIE	Large Area Crop Inventory Experiment (U.S.)
LDC	Less developed country
LSIC	Large-scale integrated (electronic) circuit
LWR	Light water (nuclear) reactor
MNC	Multinational corporation (also rendered multinational enterprise—MNE)
NASA	National Aeronautics and Space Administration (U.S.)
NATO	North Atlantic Treaty Organization
NPT	Treaty on the Non-Proliferation of Nuclear Weapons
NRC	Nuclear Regulatory Commission (U.S.)
NRDC	National Research Development Corporation (U.K.)
NSC	National Security Council (U.S.)
NSF	National Science Foundation (U.S.)
OAPEC	Organization of Arab Petroleum Exporting Countries
OAS	Organization of American States
OECD	Organisation for Economic Co-operation and Development
OES	Bureau of Oceans, International Environmental and Scientific Affairs (U.S. Department of State)
OPEC	Organization of Petroleum Exporting Countries
OST	Office of Science and Technology (U.S.)
OSTP	Office of Science and Technology Policy (U.S., successor to OST)
OTP	Office of Telecommunications Policy (U.S.)
PNE	Peaceful nuclear explosive

PNET	Treaty on Underground Nuclear Explosions for Peaceful Purposes
R&D	Research and development
S&T	Science and technology
SEATO	Southeast Asia Treaty Organization
UNCTAD	UN Conference on Trade and Development
UNDP	UN Development Program
UNEP	UN Environmental Program
UNESCO	UN Educational, Scientific and Cultural Organization
UNIDO	United Nations Industrial Development Organization
URENCO	U.K. West German and Netherlands Consortium, for uranium enrichment
WHO	World Health Organization (UN)

INDEX